Caesar
and Roman Politics
60–50 B.C.

Caesar
and Roman Politics
60–50 B.C.

by

JAMES SABBEN-CLARE

OXFORD UNIVERSITY PRESS

1971

Oxford University Press, Ely House, London W.1

GLASGOW NEW YORK TORONTO MELBOURNE WELLINGTON
CAPE TOWN SALISBURY IBADAN NAIROBI DAR ES SALAAM LUSAKA ADDIS ABABA
BOMBAY CALCUTTA MADRAS KARACHI LAHORE DACCA
KUALA LUMPUR SINGAPORE HONG KONG TOKYO

The cover shows the reverse of an aureus
of 50 B.C. with a trophy of Gallic arms. Reproduced
by permission of the Trustees of the British Museum.

1447

72-26528

Printed in Great Britain by
Robert MacLehose & Co. Ltd., The University Press, Glasgow.

Preface

Roman political history of the first century B.C. offers an unusual abundance of source-material: apart from the contemporary writing of Caesar and Cicero, there are full derivative accounts in Appian and Dio, relevant biographies by Suetonius and Plutarch, and numerous other lesser works adding their own information or interpretations. To the student or teacher this abundance may easily prove an embarrassment; even if all the material is available, the location and translation of sources is a lengthy business that cannot usually be accommodated within the limits of a school time-table. The best way of resolving this difficulty, it seems to me, is not to fall back on the standard modern text-books, but to have the sources presented in such a way that historical problems can be studied in detail by people who have neither a large classical library nor a command of classical languages. That is one of the guiding principles behind the construction of this book; another is the belief that history should be studied in terms of problems, not periods. Both of these aims are in keeping with the principles on which the JACT Ancient History syllabus has been constructed; it was in fact the demands of that syllabus, together with the lack of suitable handbooks, which first prompted me to undertake this work, and I hope that students and teachers may find that it fulfils a specific need within that context.

The bulk of this book consists of some four hundred excerpts in translation, taken from twenty or more ancient sources, with a limited amount of introductory and explanatory material. Some further information about the sources and their context is included at the end. The translations aim at clarity rather than literal reproduction of the original; only where the sense is irrecoverable or a matter for substantial dispute have I resorted to the obelisk. When I have inserted non-textual matter into the excerpts, this is placed between square brackets.

The chapters and sections are arranged thematically rather than in strict chronological sequence. At the beginning of each chapter is a brief introduction which suggests the central problem to be examined; within the chapter more specific questions are attached to the relevant excerpts or group of excerpts. Some of them can be answered very simply, some lead into the discussion of fundamental issues; for those who wish to take their investigation further, I have appended a very selective bibliography of recent works in English relevant to the main topics. As far as possible I have tried not to give my own answers — though of course some of my convictions will be apparent from my selection and arrangement of material; and the sources offered will, I hope, accommodate a broad spectrum of interpretation. The purpose of the book will have been achieved if it enables the student to form his own opinions and criticize those of others about the achievement of Julius Caesar in the important years 60–50 B.C.

The College, Winchester   J.P.S.–C.

Contents

Note:
1. All dates are B.C. unless otherwise stated.
2. The letters *B.G.* refer throughout to Caesar's Commentaries on the Gallic War.

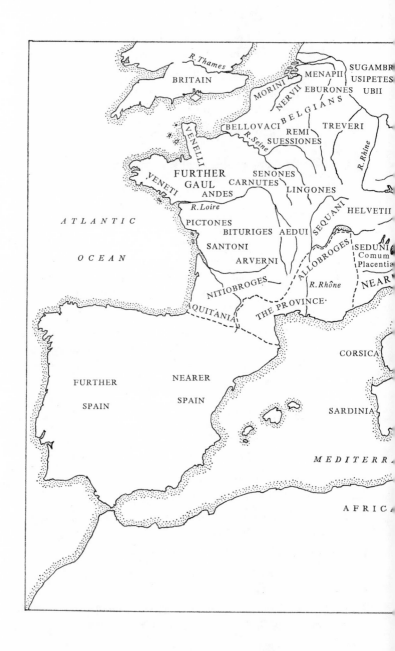

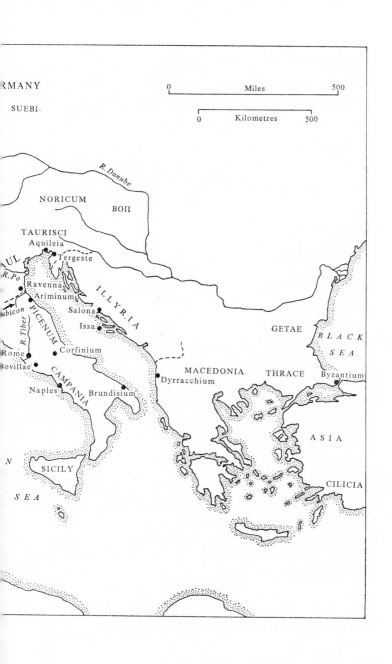

GERMANY

SUEBI·

0   Miles   500

0   Kilometres   500

R. Danube

NORICUM

BOII

TAURISCI

Aquileia

GAUL

Tergeste

R. Po

Ravenna

ILLYRIA

Ariminum

Rubicon

Salona

PICENUM

R. Tiber

Issa

Rome

Corfinium

GETAE

BLACK

SEA

Bovillae

CAMPANIA

MACEDONIA

THRACE

Byzantium

Naples

Dyrracchium

Brundisium

ASIA

SICILY

CILICIA

SEA

I. Caesar's Consulship

When Caesar returned to Rome from his Spanish province in the summer of 60, it would have been difficult to predict the impact he was going to make on Roman politics in the course of the next few months. His career so far had contained little out of the ordinary, at any rate by contemporary standards, and he had enjoyed none of the special commands which had added so much lustre to Pompey's name. This story of Plutarch may well have some truth in it:

> When he had some time to himself in Spain, he began reading a history of Alexander. He remained completely absorbed for a long while, then began weeping. His friends were astonished and asked the reason. 'Wouldn't you think it sad that at my age Alexander was already king of such a great empire, while I have not got anything to my credit?' (Plutarch *Caesar* 11.3).

Such political support as he had hitherto commanded was from the lower classes of society, whose favour he had bought by lavish expenditure on games, banquets, public works, and festivals (Plutarch *Caesar* 5). It was only during his consulship that he began to emerge as a political figure of more than ordinary importance. The excerpts in this chapter attempt to show how he set about accumulating his remarkable power and influence in the years 60 and 59. (For more detailed discussion of the significance of Caesar's consulship, see Bibliography.)

A. The situation in Rome before Caesar's consulship

POMPEY AND CATO

The leading personality in Rome was Pompey, recently returned from his triumphant campaigns against Mithridates in Asia. However his attempts to capitalize on his military successes were thwarted by a Senate wary of putting too much power into the hands of one man. Their leading spokesman, M. Porcius Cato, made it clear that he would not compromise his conservative principles to serve Pompey's interests.

1.

PLUTARCH *Pomp.* 44 (1) As the law did not permit him to enter the city before his triumph, Pompey sent a request to the Senate that the consular election be put off as a favour, so that he could lend his personal assistance to Piso's candidature. (2) But Cato opposed the request and prevented him getting what he wanted. Pompey was struck by his outspokenness and his firm adherence to moral principles which only he was prepared to adopt in public, and so determined to win him over somehow. As Cato had two nieces, Pompey proposed marrying one himself, and giving the other in marriage to his son. (3) Cato was suspicious of the idea, seeing in it an attempt to bribe him by means of a marriage alliance; his wife and sister however were distressed at the prospect of throwing away the kinship of Pompey the Great.

> This Piso was Marcus Pupius Piso Calpurnianus, who had served on Pompey's staff for the last six years, and had been sent on by him to stand for the consulship of 61.

2.

PLUTARCH *Cat. Min.* 30 (4) [Cato's reply to Pompey's proposal:] 'Go and tell Pompey that Cato is not to be hooked by way of the women's quarters. He acknowledges Pompey's goodwill, and is prepared to offer friendship firmer than any marriage connexion if Pompey's behaviour is honest; but he will not give hostages for the glory of Pompey against the interests of the country . . .' (6) If we are to judge by the results, Cato seems to have been quite wrong not to accept the match, since it left Pompey to turn to Caesar and contract a marriage which united their powers and nearly overthrew the constitution and destroyed the state.

> For the marriage referred to in (6), see no. **12**. Was it as important as Plutarch suggests? See nos. **144, 251** ff.

> The consuls of 61 proved a disappointment to Pompey, and he was compelled to use his influence to have another pair of his own choosing elected for the next year.

3.

DIO 37.49 (1) Pompey had Lucius Afranius and [Q. Caecilius] Metellus Celer appointed consuls [for the year 60] in the vain hope that he would be able to accomplish whatever he wanted through them. (2) His main requirements were that some land be given to his soldiers, and that all his 'acts' be ratified; but at the time he failed to secure either. The *optimates* who had never been on friendly terms with him prevented a vote being taken; (3) as for the consuls, Afranius knew more about dancing than business, and was no use to him at all. Metellus was embittered because his sister had been divorced by Pompey in spite of bearing him children, and opposed him in everything . . . 50 (5) So when Pompey found that he could do nothing because of Metellus and the rest, he said that they were jealous of him, and that he would put the matter before the plebs. But fearing that they would also fail him and make his shame even greater, he abandoned his claims. (6) So he discovered that he really had no power at all; his name and past reputation only made people envious, and brought him no profit whatsoever.

> These 'acts' were the administrative arrangements he had left behind in his province. They required ratification by the Senate. For the characteristics of the *optimates*, see Cic. *Sest.* 136 ff.

4.

PLUTARCH *Cat. Min.* 31 (1) When Pompey and [L. Licinius] Lucullus fell into argument over the arrangements in Pontus (each claiming that his own 'acts' should be ratified), Cato sided with Lucullus who was manifestly the aggrieved party [cf. no. 14]; Pompey was defeated in the Senate and turned to the people, trying to get a land distribution for his soldiers. (2) But Cato successfully opposed this law as well, and drove Pompey to attach himself to Clodius, the most outspoken of the popular leaders, and to seek the support of Caesar. To some extent Cato was initially responsible for this.

> For Clodius' political career, see Index.

FACTIONS IN ROME

The other leading individuals in Rome were M. Licinius Crassus (consul with Pompey in 70) and M. Tullius Cicero (consul in 63). Crassus had been rather overshadowed by the achievements of Pompey, and there had long been bad blood between them; his financial enterprises gave him a bond with the Knights, who were at the moment trying unsuccessfully to obtain from the Senate a revision of the contract for collecting taxes in Asia. Cicero still imagined himself to be bathed in the glory of his consulship, when he had used drastic measures to put down the threatened conspiracy of Catiline; he also had great admiration for Pompey, whom he looked to as the champion of his own political causes.

5.

CICERO *ad Att.* 1.17 [Rome, 5 Dec. 61] (8) We live in a state that is weak, wretched and unstable. I expect you have heard that our friends the Knights have almost split from the Senate; first they were very annoyed at the promulgation of a senatorial decree to the effect that any who had received bribes as jurymen should be liable to prosecution. I happened not to be present when the decree was made, but felt that the Knights, without openly saying so, were not at all pleased. So I delivered to the Senate what I thought to be a highly authoritative rebuke and, although my case was not a very respectable one, made my point with some weight and at some length. (9) And here's another nice piece of work by the Knights! It's almost intolerable; and yet I have not only tolerated it, but graced it with my support. The contractors who bought up the tax-collecting rights in Asia have complained to the Senate that their cupidity led them to overbid. They have asked that the contract be rescinded. I was in the front line of their support, or rather the second, for it is Crassus who has put them up to making this audacious demand. It's a tricky business. The demand is scandalous, and simply shows up their recklessness. But if they don't get what they want, they really will be at odds with the Senate; that's the main danger.

6.

CICERO *ad Att.* 1.18 [Rome, 20 Jan. 60] (5) Metellus [cf. no. **3**] is an excellent consul, and devoted to me; but he has undermined his authority by having made, for the sake of appearances, the same proposal about Clodius [see nos. **33** ff.]. But as for Afranius, heavens! What a gutless, witless warrior! . . . (6) An agrarian law has been proposed by Flavius; not much in it of course — it's much the same as Plotius' bill [cf. no. **8**]. But in the meantime there is no one with any idea of statesmanship to be found. One who might have had — Pompey, my dear friend (for so he is, I'd like you to know) — he just keeps silence out of respect for that pretty embroidered robe of his. Crassus hasn't said anything to offend. The others you know: they're such fools that they still think they can keep their fishponds safe even if the Republic is lost. (7) There is Cato of course, and he is a man apart. But his concern is manifested more by his high-principled integrity than by his wits or policies; he has been harassing the wretched tax-collectors, who were once his greatest friends, for two months, and won't allow the Senate to give them an answer.

> The bill of Flavius was another unsuccessful attempt to get land voted to Pompey's veterans. Nothing definite is known about the law of Plotius. Pompey's embroidered robe had been one of the honours voted him in 63 at the instigation of Caesar.

7.

PLUTARCH *Crass.* 7 (2) Crassus, giving up any attempt to equal the military achievements of Pompey, plunged into politics, and by his energy and readiness to plead a cause, lend money, and assist candidates for office by campaigning and canvassing on their behalf, he acquired influence and reputation no less than Pompey had won from his great campaigns. (3) The circumstances of each were different; Pompey's name and power in the city were increased by his absence, because of his campaigns; when he was in Rome, he was often outshone by Crassus, because the pomp and circumstance of his life made him keep away from the crowds and avoid the forum. His assistance was given sparingly to others, and with no great enthusiasm, as he preferred to keep his resources in good trim for his own use. (4) Crassus on the other hand was always ready to offer his services, open-handed and approachable; always actively engaged in some enterprise, he achieved more by his liberality and kindness than Pompey did by standing on his dignity. . . . (7) And when the whole of Rome was split into three parties, those of Pompey, Caesar, and Crassus (Cato's reputation was greater than his actual power, and he won more admiration than support), the sensible conservative element in the city cultivated Pompey, the fickle impulsive element followed Caesar's hopes, (8) while Crassus adopted a middle course and drew support from both sides. He frequently changed his political ideas, and

was neither a reliable friend nor an implacable enemy, but readily
redirected his favours and animosities as his interests required.
This meant that he often appeared as both the advocate and the
opponent of the same men or measures. (9) His favours won him
considerable influence, but the fear which he inspired no less.

Compare this picture of Crassus with that given by Dio in no. **13** and
by Florus in no. **16**.

8.

CICERO *ad Att.* 2.1 [Antium, June 60] (6) You ask about the
agrarian law [cf. no. **6**]. Well, it seems to be on ice at the moment.
As for your gentle dig at me for my friendship with Pompey, I
wouldn't like you to think that I took his side for my own protection. No, the position is such that, if there should be any breach
between us, the state would inevitably be involved in deep factional
division. But the precautions and provisions that I have taken do
not mean that I am abandoning my conservative principles,
merely that he has become more sympathetic to this policy, and
has more or less given up his irresponsible pursuit of popularity. . . .
What if I could get Caesar on our side as well, now that the wind
sits so fair for him? That wouldn't be a disservice to the state,
would it? (7) And supposing I had no detractors, but only the
universal support that is my due, even then wouldn't it be preferable to offer a remedy which cures the diseased limbs of the state
rather than amputates them? But now, as things are, the Knights
. . . have deserted the Senate; our leading citizens think they are
in heaven if the bearded mullets in their fishponds will feed from
their hands, and are not interested in anything else. So won't I be
doing some good if I can dissuade from causing trouble those who
are capable of it? (8) As for Cato, my affection for him is no less
than yours; but even with the best will in the world, there are
times when his high-mindedness is a positive danger to the state.
He delivers opinions which would be more at home in the pages
of Plato's Republic than among the dregs of Romulus here. If a
juryman is bribed, he should be liable to prosecution himself; that's
a fair enough principle. It won the vote of Cato and the approval
of the Senate; but the result — alienation of the Knights. Not
from me, mind you. I was against it. Again it was scandalous that

the tax-collectors should ask for a revision of their contract. But for the sake of retaining their goodwill we should have been prepared to accept the loss. Cato took a stand against it and won the day. The result — a consul imprisoned and rioting at large; and not a whisper from any of those whose support I and my consular successors used to rely on to defend the state. 'Well then' you say, 'shall we get them onto our side by bribery?' That may be the only expedient.

> The consul imprisoned was Metellus Celer, who resisted the proposals of Flavius so uncompromisingly that the exasperated tribune had him locked up (cf. no. **67**). The consul had a hole broken in the wall, and called the Senate to meet him there, until Pompey told Flavius to desist.
>
> What political principles can be attributed to Cicero on the basis of what he writes here and in no. **6**? How fair is his criticism of Cato (cf. nos. **1, 2**)?

It is arguable that Caesar would not have made such an immediate impact on Roman politics had the state been less 'wretched' and 'unstable' (no. **7**). What was the reason for this weakness? Plutarch's account emphasizes the clash between the leading personalities whereas Cicero's letters indicate larger forces in conflict. Does this just reflect a difference in interest between the two authors, or is one interpretation definitely to be preferred? If there were 'parties' involved, how were they constituted? Were they groups of people sharing similar ideals, or were they the personal adherents of individual politicians?

B. Caesar's election as consul

THE ELECTIONS

At the expense of the triumph for which he had qualified in Spain, Caesar secured his election as consul for the year 59 by liberal use of other people's money.

9.

APPIAN *B.C.* 2.8 (28) The Senate awarded him a triumph, and he set about making preparations for a procession on the most splendid scale just outside the walls of Rome. This coincided with the days during which candidates for the consulship had to present themselves; this had to be done in person, but once a man had entered the city, he could not go back for a triumph. (29) As Caesar was particularly anxious for office and his procession was not yet ready, he sent a request to the Senate that he should be given permission to present himself for the consulship in absence, and that his friends should stand in for him. This was against the law, as he knew, but there were precedents for it. (30) Cato however opposed the request and took up the whole of the day for the presentation of the candidates with filibustering. So Caesar abandoned his triumph and entered the city. He presented himself as a candidate and waited for the elections.

C. Marius had been elected consul in absence for the years 104, 103 and 101.

10.

SUETONIUS *Div. Jul.* 18 (2) The day for the elections had been already announced and his candidature could not be accepted unless he entered the city as a private citizen. As there was considerable opposition to his attempts to get round the law, he was compelled to give up his triumph, to avoid being debarred from the consulship. 19 (1) There were two other candidates, Lucius Lucceius and Marcus [Calpurnius] Bibulus. Caesar joined forces with Lucceius on the understanding that Lucceius, with less influence but more money to his credit, should bribe the electorate in the name of them both. When the *optimates* came to hear of this, they were worried that there would be no holding Caesar if he were elected to the consulship with an amenable and co-operative colleague. So they authorized Bibulus to match his bribery; most of them contributed from their own pockets, and even Cato admitted that bribery in such circumstances was for the good of the state. (2) So Caesar was elected consul with Bibulus.

11.

DIO 37.54 (3) As Caesar had high hopes of success, he did not object to giving up his triumph, but entered the city to present his candidature. Even though Pompey and Crassus were still at odds with each other and had their own political following; even though each of them opposed whatever he saw the other wanted, Caesar worked on them — and everyone else — so skilfully that he won their support and was unanimously elected by them all.

THE PARTNERSHIP OF CAESAR, POMPEY, AND CRASSUS

The Republican constitution was designed to limit the amount of influence any one politician could exercise. However families and individuals had long been able to strengthen their position by a system of patronage and political alliances (cf. nos. 1, 2). So Caesar set about winning the cooperation of both Pompey and Crassus in a partnership that is sometimes called 'The First Triumvirate'. His side of the bargain was to provide what the Senate had refused to consent to — for Pompey, a land-grant to accommodate his veterans and confirmation of his settlement of Asia (cf. nos. 3, 4); for Crassus, a revision of the Asian tax-contract as the Knights demanded (cf. no. 5). They in return were to support him with money, votes, and influence.

12.

VELLEIUS 2.44 (1) In Caesar's consulship the partnership of power was formed between himself, Pompey, and Crassus; its results were to be ruinous for the city, the world and even, at different times, for each of themselves. (2) Pompey's reason for being a party to it was that he hoped to obtain through Caesar's influence as consul the ratification of his 'acts' in the overseas provinces, to which many objections were still being made. Caesar realized that he would add to his own prestige by making this concession to Pompey's and by letting him carry the weight of unpopularity for their partnership he would strengthen his own position. Crassus hoped that the influence of Pompey and the power of Caesar would enable him to attain the position of pre-eminence which he had not managed to reach on his own. (3) As an additional bond, Caesar and Pompey entered a marriage alliance, with Pompey taking to wife Julia, Caesar's daughter.

13.

DIO 37.55 (1) Caesar reconciled Pompey and Crassus, not because he wanted them to agree, but because he saw that they were the most powerful people and realized that he would not be able to achieve much without the assistance of both, or at any rate one of them; and if he joined forces with either of them alone, he would automatically antagonize the other and lose more through him than he would gain from the other's support . . . 56 (3) Pompey was not as strong as he hoped: the power of Crassus and the growing influence of Caesar made him afraid that they would eclipse him completely and led him to hope that if he went into partnership with them now they would help him to regain his old authority. (4) Crassus thought that his family and wealth gave him a claim to pre-eminence; and because he was quite outshone by Pompey and saw Caesar on the way to greatness, he hoped to set them against each other so that neither should get the upper hand. Well-matched antagonists as they were, he expected to be able to profit from the friendship of each of them and outstrip them both in honours. (5) He did not commit himself unreservedly to the policies of either people or Senate, but acted in whatever way was likely to advance his own personal cause.

14.

APPIAN *B.C.* 2.9 (31) Pompey had won great distinction and power in his Mithridatic wars and now made repeated requests for the Senate to ratify the numerous grants he had conferred on kings, chieftains, and cities. (32) But most of the Senators demurred out of jealousy. Prominent among them was Lucullus, who had been campaigning against Mithridates beforehand and considered that his own arrangements ought to stand as he had left Mithridates to Pompey in a thoroughly weakened state. (33) Crassus sided with Lucullus and this drove the indignant Pompey to Caesar's side. In return for Pompey's oath to assist him to the consulship, Caesar immediately reconciled him to Crassus and so these three very powerful men made common cause. The author Varro wrote a book about this partnership, called 'Tricaranus' [The Three-Headed Monster].

15.

SUETONIUS *Div. Jul.* 19 (2) The three of them were thus brought into partnership, on the understanding that no political action should be taken which did not suit any one of the three.

16.

FLORUS 2.13 (9) Cato, who always had a grudge against the holders of power, began to decry Pompey and fulminate against his 'acts'. This antagonized the indignant Pompey and drove him to seek protection for his status. (10) This happened to coincide with the peak of Crassus' fortunes, based on nobility of birth, riches and high office, although his appetite for wealth was still unsated. Caesar was on his way up, thanks to his eloquence and dynamic personality, besides his present consulship; but Pompey was still the most distinguished of the three. (11) So they readily agreed to make an assault on the constitution because each had similar desires for power, although Caesar was anxious to achieve status, Crassus to increase his, and Pompey to hold onto his.

Before the end of the year Caesar had begun to canvass for the agrarian law he intended to introduce.

17.

CICERO *ad Att.* 2.3 [Antium, Dec. 60] (3) We must either firmly oppose this agrarian law — that would involve us in some fighting, but plenty of credit — or keep quiet, which is much the same as going off to Solonium or Antium; or of course we could support it, and people say this is what Caesar confidently expects. For Cornelius has been here — Balbus I should say, Caesar's friend. He assured me that Caesar would consult me and Pompey on everything and would do what he could to reconcile Crassus with Pompey. If I do go along with it, the advantages are these: a close link with Pompey, even with Caesar too, if I want it; a return to good relations with my enemies; peace with the plebs and an untroubled old age.

But Cicero goes on to say that he prefers to take as his motto a line of Homer (*Iliad* 12.243): 'One omen is best, to fight for fatherland'. Why should Caesar have wanted to keep on good terms with Cicero (cf. nos. **30, 31**)?

The term 'triumvirate' properly means a commission of three, appointed for a specific purpose (e.g. for minting coins or for distributing land); in 43 Octavian, Antony, and Lepidus — the so-called Second Triumvirate — were similarly appointed 'to put the state in order'. Why then is it misleading to call the partnership of Caesar, Pompey, and Crassus 'The First Triumvirate'? How did Crassus and Pompey differ from Caesar in status, and what did they stand to gain by supporting him? What guarantee did Caesar have that they would not join forces against him?

C. Caesar's consulship

THE AGRARIAN LAWS

Within a month of entering office Caesar had acquired a formidable body
of support. He used this to carry his first and most important piece of
legislation, an agrarian law to distribute to the poor some of the land in
Italy owned by the state. No doubt this could be justified on social
grounds alone, but it was also an obvious way to win political support
from the lower classes. Caesar's conservative opponents, suspicious of his
ulterior motives, prepared to thwart him with every constitutional means
at their disposal. He was more than a match for them and showed himself
ready to use chicanery, threats and even violence to get his own way.

18.

DIO 38.1 (1) The next year [59] Caesar was prepared to bestow
favours on the whole people, so as to bring them more firmly to
his side. But such was his anxiety to avoid the enmity of the
optimates that he wished to give the appearance of taking their side
and repeatedly assured them that he would not propose any
measures which were not in their interests as well. (2) And in fact
he so presented his first bill about the land, which he intended to
distribute to the whole population, that no fault was found with it
at all. . . . 2 (2) Nevertheless practically all the *optimates* who were
outside the partnership were very disgruntled, especially as the
law had been so framed as to be impossible to fault, even though
it was to the disadvantage of them all. (3) They suspected — quite
justifiably — that the bill was designed to attach the people to him
and to give him a reputation and influence above anyone else. So
even though no one spoke against it, they did not express their
approval either. 3 (1) Cato however urged on general grounds that
they should keep to the present arrangement and not go outside it,
even though not even he could find specific points in the bill to
attack. . . . (2) At this Caesar made as if to have Cato dragged out of
the Senate House and thrown into prison. But Cato showed a great
readiness to be removed and a number of others followed him,
including Marcus Petreius. When Petreius was rebuked by Caesar
for leaving before the Senate had been dismissed, he replied 'I
would rather be in prison with Cato than stay here with you.' This
shamed Caesar into letting Cato go free. . . . 4 (1) After that he

brought no further business before the Senate during his year of office, but referred directly to the people anything that he wanted. (2) However as he still wished to have the support of the leading Senators . . . he began by asking his colleague Bibulus whether he disapproved of the provisions of the law. . . . (3) and prevailed on the people to join him in the request, saying to them 'You will have the law if Bibulus is willing.' To this Bibulus replied loudly 'You won't have the law this year even if you all want it.' (4) Caesar did not go on to ask any of the other magistrates in case they too should oppose him, but called forward Pompey and Crassus although they held no office, and told them to give their opinion of the proposals. . . . 5 (3) [When Pompey had spoken in favour of the bill,] Caesar asked him if he would be ready to help against the opposition and urged the people to join in the request. (4) Pompey was delighted at the idea of both the consul and the people soliciting his support even though he held no command, and so spoke at length with a great show of dignity and self-importance, ending with the words 'If anyone dares to raise a sword, then I too will take up my shield.' (5) Crassus too approved of what Pompey had said.

For Caesar's arrangements about provincial commands for the following year, see the next chapter.

19.

APPIAN *B.C.* 2.10 (35) Caesar was adept at the art of dissimulation and made speeches in the Senate about sharing the views of Bibulus, saying that the State would suffer if they fell out. Bibulus took him at his word and had no idea what was in the wind. While he was unprepared and off his guard, Caesar collected a large gang of partisans and brought before the Senate a bill to help the poor by distributing land to them.

20.

DIO 38.6 (1) Bibulus still would not give in and continued to obstruct the passage of the bill with the help of three sympathetic tribunes. Finally when no other pretext for delay remained, he proclaimed a 'sacred period' for all the remaining days of the year, which made it legally impossible for the people even to convene an assembly. (2) Caesar paid little attention and fixed a day for the passage of the law. The people had occupied the forum during the night, when Bibulus came up with his supporters and forced his way into the Temple of Castor from which Caesar was speaking. The audience made way for him, partly out of respect, (3) partly because they did not expect any opposition from him; but when he got up and tried to speak, he was pushed down the steps. . . .

Further indignities suffered by Bibulus:

21.

PLUTARCH *Pomp.* 48 (1) His lictors had their *fasces* broken, two of the tribunes who accompanied him were wounded, and he had a basket of manure emptied over his head. (2) When the people had cleared the forum of their opponents, they passed the law about the distribution of the land.

Cicero's comment on Atticus' account of the passing of the law:

22.

CICERO *ad Att.* 2.15 [Formiae, c. 29 April 59] (2) Bibulus shows great spirit in trying to hold up the Assembly, but it is nothing more than an expression of his feelings and does not do anything to help the state. There is no doubt that Publius is our only hope. Let's have him as tribune by all means.

> This Publius was P. Clodius who was trying to get himself transferred to the plebs so that he could be elected tribune. See nos. **33** ff.

23

PLUTARCH *Caes.* 14 (6) Since Bibulus made no headway in trying to obstruct Caesar's laws, but with Cato often ran the risk of losing his life in the forum, he stayed shut up at home for the rest of his year of office. Pompey however filled the forum with soldiers immediately after his marriage and joined in the popular support for the laws.

24.

DIO 38.6 (5) Bibulus remained at home and, whenever Caesar was bringing in a new proposal, he sent notice through his attendants that it was a 'sacred period' and, legally speaking, Caesar had no right to do any business during it. (6) A tribune, Publius Vatinius, threatened to put Bibulus in prison for this, but the opposition of his colleagues persuaded him to desist.

25.

PLUTARCH *Cat. Min.* 32 (3) Besides the land-law being passed, a clause was added that all the Senate had to swear an oath to recognize the law and to help against anyone who opposed it. Heavy penalties were laid down for non-compliance. Everyone took the oath under compulsion . . . [For a time Cato refused.] (4) It was Cicero who was responsible for getting him to take the oath . . . (6) and in the end he was prevailed upon and came forward to take the oath last of all, but for Favonius, one of his friends and associates.

> An oath-sanction of this kind was not new: it had been used by the tribune Saturninus in the year 100 for another piece of agrarian legislation — and had caused the same resentment.

The new law was administered by a Commission of Twenty; there was also an inner Commission of Five, probably Caesar's friends. The following is from an inscription, called an *elogium*, recording the political career of one of its members.

26.

I.L.S. 46. Marcus Valerius, son of Marcus, grandson of Manius / Messalla, chief priest, / twice military tribune, quaestor, city praetor, consul [in 61], / Member of the Commission of Five for giving, assigning and adjudicating land-grants, / three times *Interrex*, Censor.

Towards the end of April, when all effective opposition had been silenced, Caesar promulgated a second land-law, designed to distribute the rich Campanian country which had been specifically excluded from the terms of the first bill.

27.

CICERO *ad Att.* 2.16 [Formiae, April 59] (2) What our friend Gnaius [Pompey] is up to, I simply have no idea. . . . He has been deliberately evasive so far, saying that he approves of Caesar's legislation, but is bound to leave the responsibility of implementing it to Caesar. He said he had been in favour of the agrarian law, but it was no concern of his whether or not there was a possibility of vetoing it. He had been in favour of settling that business with the King of Egypt at last, but saw no reason to ask whether or not Bibulus had been 'observing the signs from heaven' at the time. As for the tax-collectors, he had been happy to oblige the Knights, but could not have foreseen what would happen to Bibulus if he chose to go into the forum at that moment. Well, Sampsiceramus, what are you going to say now? . . . Perhaps, 'I'll use Caesar's army to keep you under my thumb.'

> The Egyptian king was Ptolemy Auletes, who paid enormous sums to Caesar to have his position ratified (Cic. *Rab. Post.* 6). Sampsiceramus was a pet-name for Pompey. 'Caesar's army' has been thought to refer loosely to his numerous partisans: or more specifically to the troops voted to him for his Gallic campaigns (cf. nos. **72** ff.). Is this picture of Pompey consistent with that given in nos. **18, 23**?

THE AREAS OF SUPPORT FOR CAESAR

Caesar's legislation effectively won him the sympathy of all classes except the Senate. Reluctant to be dissociated from the conservative element altogether, he continued to make overtures to Cicero whose attitude however remained ambivalent.

28.

PLUTARCH *Caes.* 14 (8) Of the other Senators (besides Cato) only a very few continued to go with Caesar to the Senate. The rest stayed away to show their disapproval.

29.

DIO 38.7 (4) By means of these laws Caesar attached the people to his side; the Knights he won by remitting a third of their tax-collecting contract. . . . (5) When Caesar had accommodated this class without a word of protest being raised, he went on to ratify

all the 'acts' of Pompey, with no opposition from Lucullus or anyone else, and then passed many other measures unopposed.

30.

CICERO *ad Att.* 2.18 [Rome, c. June 59] (3) Caesar has very
generously offered me a post on his staff, as well as a Free Commission to discharge a vow. But the latter does not provide enough
protection, Little Beauty's sense of respect being what it is, and it
also prevents me being here to meet my brother. The former is
safe and doesn't stop me being here when I want. It's mine for the
taking, but I don't think I shall use it. Still, no one knows. Running
away doesn't appeal to me: I want to fight. I have plenty of support.
But I'm not committing myself and I hope you'll keep quiet about
this.

> A 'Free Commission' gave the holder all the perquisites of an ambas-
> sador without any of the responsibilities. Cicero disapproved of them
> in principle (*Laws* 3.8.18) and had tried during his consulship to get
> them abolished. 'Little Beauty' refers to Clodius and is derived from
> his last name, *Pulcher*.

This is how, four years later, Cicero described his relations with Caesar
in 59:

31.

CICERO *Prov. Cos.* 41. As consul he did a number of things in
which he wanted me to take part. I could not approve of them,
but I was bound to feel pleased at the opinion he had of me. He
asked me to be a member of the Commission of Five [cf. no. **26**];
he wanted to include me in a group of three very close associates
of consular rank [cf. no. **17**]; he offered me any embassy I wanted.
But I turned down every offer, not from ingratitude, but as a
matter of rigid principle.

The Vettius Conspiracy, a strange affair perhaps intended to win sympathy
for Pompey (see Bibliography):

32.

CICERO *ad Att.* 2.24 [Rome, c. Aug. 59] (2) It looks as if our old
friend Vettius the informer promised Caesar that he would arrange

for young Curio [cf. no. **40**] to fall under suspicion of criminal conduct. He wormed his way into the young man's company and, as the evidence shows, went about with him constantly. Finally he brought matters to a head by telling Curio that he had arranged a plot with his slaves to attack Pompey and kill him. . . . [However Curio did not agree to join in. Instead he told his father who in turn told Pompey and the whole matter came out into the open. Vettius was called upon to make a statement in the Senate, and another the next day in the forum.] (3) . . . There he gave the names of a number of people on whom not even a breath of suspicion had fallen in the Senate — Lucullus, who, he said, had sent Gaius Fannius, the junior prosecuting counsel in the Clodius case; and Lucius Domitius [cf. nos. **49**ff.] from whose house it had been planned to make the attack, so he said. The general opinion was that Vettius hoped to arrange to be arrested in the forum with his slaves carrying weapons and then offer to turn informer. That is what would have happened if the Curios had not told Pompey all about it first.

THE ADOPTION OF CLODIUS INTO THE PLEBS

The tribunate with its powers of obstructing and initiating legislation was of great importance and a sympathetic tribune was a valuable asset to any politician. Caesar's main tribunician agent was Publius Clodius who had been trying since the beginning of 60 to exchange his patrician status (he belonged to the aristocratic Claudius Pulcher family) for plebeian. Clodius emerges as a devious, turbulent character and it is difficult to know where he stands politically. Cicero at first thought he was anti-Caesarian; but even if this were so, we do not know whether he was acting in self-interest, or perhaps on behalf of Crassus, as often we are at the mercy of the evidence of Cicero whose attitude could not help being coloured by personal animosity.

33.
CICERO *ad Att.* 1.18 [Rome, 20 Jan. 60] (4) There's a tribune called Gaius Herennius . . . well, he has been trying to get Clodius transferred to the plebs . . . I treated him in my usual way in the Senate, but the man is peculiarly insensitive.

> The matter was debated in the Senate in June, but the attempt failed (*ad Att.* 2.1.5). By the following year Cicero's attitude had changed (cf. no. **22**).

34.

CICERO *ad Att.* 2.7 [Antium, April 59] (3) You know, our friend Clodius is getting a pretty raw deal: once he was number one in Caesar's household, now he hasn't even got a place on the Commission of Twenty; and first he was promised one commission, then given a different one.

In view of what happened later to Cicero (see nos. 53 ff.), he changed his mind again about Clodius, as shown in a speech made immediately after his return from exile in August 57.

35.

CICERO *Dom.* 41. It must have been about noon when, in the course of defending my colleague Antonius, I made some querulous remarks about the state of the Republic, which seemed to have some bearing on the poor man's condition. Certain worthy gentlemen at once had my words reported to them, in garbled and distorted form, by their villainous informants. By three o'clock that same day you had been adopted into the plebs. Of course if three hours is long enough in the case of adoptions, although three weeks notice is required before a bill can be voted on, then I have no objection.

Antonius had been Cicero's colleague as consul in 63; Cicero had won his co-operation by seeing that he got the rich province of Macedonia. He was however a poor and unsuccessful governor and on his return was prosecuted for maladministration, although there were also darker suspicions of his complicity with Catiline. Cicero defended him, unsuccessfully and against Caesar's wishes.

36.

CICERO *ad Att.* 2.12 [Three Taverns, 19 April 59] (1) Deny that Publius has been made a plebeian? Do they indeed? There's real tyranny for you! It's intolerable. Let Publius send me some witnesses, and I'll declare on oath that our friend Gnaius [Pompey] was present at the auspices, on his own admission . . . (2) Now here's a coincidence; I had just left the Antium district and joined the Appian way at Three Taverns — this was on Ceres' day — when along came my friend Curio from Rome. At the very same

moment a boy appeared with letters from you. Curio asked whether
I had heard the news. 'No' I said. 'Publius is seeking election as a
tribune.' 'No, really?' 'Yes, and he's Caesar's deadly enemy and
means to rescind all the new bills.' 'What does Caesar think of this?'
'He says he had nothing to do with proposing Clodius' adoption
into the plebs.'

37.

CICERO *ad Att.* 2.19 [Rome, early July 59] (1) I have many causes
for concern, arising both from this great political upheaval and
from the dangers which threaten me personally . . . (4) Our friend
Publius is hostile and has made repeated threats. Things will soon
come to a head and I shall expect you to hurry back. Anyway I
think I have still got a good strong consular army behind me,
made up of all the men who have at least got some principles.
Pompey shows signs of being more than ordinarily considerate to
me. He says Clodius will not say a word about me; but he can't
deceive me and is in fact deceived himself.

> Cicero repeats Pompey's assurances in two letters written the same
> month (*ad Att.* 2.20.2, 2.31.6).

38.

CICERO *ad Att.* 2.22 [Rome, August 59] (1) When Clodius sees
how unpopular the present regime is, he makes as if to attack its
authors; but when he remembers their powerful resources and
armies, he turns against the 'good' men. I myself have been threatened with violence and legal proceedings. (2) Pompey had words
with him, and strong words too (as he told me himself, though I
have no other evidence for it). He said that if I was in any danger
from a man whose transference to the plebs had depended on his
own armed support, then he himself would get a very bad name as
a treacherous rogue . . . He claimed that Clodius had protested
volubly at first, but finally gave way and undertook not to act
against Pompey's wishes in anything. Even so he continued to use
the most offensive language about me. I wouldn't have trusted him
even if he did stop and would still have carried on with the preparations which I am now making.

POPULAR OPINION OF THE REGIME

Cicero gives a lurid picture of the hostility felt towards the regime, although it is worth noting that most of this is directed against Pompey and not Caesar. This may just be an indication of Cicero's disappointment in Pompey, or perhaps the result of a policy of deliberate self-effacement by Caesar (cf. no. 12).

39.

CICERO *ad Att.* 2.13 [Formiae, c. 24 April 59] (2) You say that men are keeping quiet at Rome. I thought as much. Still, they are certainly not in the country. The very fields cannot abide this tyranny. I tell you, if you come to Formiae, my goodness! The protesting voices, the indignation, the hatred of our Great Friend [Pompey], whose title is now as out of date as that of Crassus — the Rich!

40.

CICERO *ad Att.* 2.18 [Rome, c. June 59] (1) We are boxed in on all sides; we don't mind this slavery so much as the fear of death and eviction, even though they are really lesser evils. But no one lifts a hand or voice in protest against this state of affairs, even though the dissatisfaction is universal. I suppose the aim of those in power is to leave nothing for anyone else to give away. The only one to speak and come out in opposition is young [C. Scribonius] Curio. He is widely applauded, greeted with great respect in the forum and treated to many other marks of approval from decent citizens. Fufius on the other hand [one of the praetors] is pursued with catcalls and shouts of abuse. I'm not really encouraged by this, rather saddened that the citizens should be so free in expression, but so limited in courage.

41.

CICERO *ad Att.* 2.19 [Rome, July 59] (2) It's a fact that the present regime is the most scandalous in history, the most disgraceful and universally hated by all sorts, classes, and ages of man. It quite exceeds my expectations, let alone my hopes. The *populares* have even taught sober citizens how to hiss . . . (3) You can get the best idea of popular sentiment from the theatres and shows. . . . At the games of Apollo the actor Diphilus weighed into Pompey merci-

lessly, and there were hundreds of encores for 'Thou art Great in
our afflictions . . .'. When Caesar came in, there was a deathly hush.
Then young Curio appeared and he was given the sort of ovation
that Pompey used to get in the good old days. Caesar was not
pleased. A letter is said to be on its way to Pompey in Capua.

42.
CICERO *ad Att.* 2.20 [Rome, July 59] (3) Public esteem and sympathy have lifted Bibulus to the skies. His edicts and speeches are
in wide circulation. It's a new pathway to glory he's found.

43.
SUETONIUS *Div. Jul.* 20 (2) From that time on, Caesar managed
all the affairs of state by himself just as he pleased. This led to
witty remarks by people who had documents to sign, adding as a
joke the declaration that the business had been transacted in the
consulship not of Caesar and Bibulus, but of Julius and Caesar.
And these lines were on everyone's lips:

> 'In Caesar's recent consulship events were happening —
> Of Bibulus' consulship I can't recall a thing.'

In substance the domestic legislation of Caesar was not so important as
his provincial arrangements (see next chapter); there is even some
difference of opinion between the sources about what it was intended to
achieve. Compare the interpretations put upon it by Dio (nos. **18, 29**)
and by Appian (no. **19**). Of more lasting importance was the manner in
which the legislation was passed, in defiance of omens, senatorial opposition, and public animosity. Why was Caesar prepared to risk incurring
such unpopularity, and what significance did his behaviour have for the
future of Republican government? Was it really the case, as Suetonius
says (no. **43**), that 'he managed all the affairs of state by himself, just as
he wished'?

D. Caesar's arrangements for the immediate political future

THE ELECTION OF MAGISTRATES FOR 58

It was easy enough for Caesar to over-ride senatorial opposition while he
himself held office in Italy and his own personal future was secured by the
five-year provincial command which forms the subject of the next chapter.

But it was dangerous to leave all the initiative to his opponents, especially when so many had been offended by the events of his consulship. Presumably he could still look to the support of Pompey and Crassus — conditional upon the amount he could continue to offer them in return — but he did not, as was expected, make them consuls. The magistrates finally elected were even thought by Cicero to be loyal to the constitution, in spite of the fact that one of the new consuls had been Pompey's lieutenant and the other was Caesar's father-in-law.

44.

CICERO *ad. Att.* 2.5 [Antium, April 59] (2) I look forward to hearing from you . . . who is being groomed for the consulship. Is it Pompey and Crassus, as popularly rumoured, or, as I have been told, Servius Sulpicius along with Gabinius?

> Sulpicius Galba had been in Transalpine Gaul under Pomptinus and accompanied Caesar there again in 58.

45.

CICERO *ad Att.* 2.21 [Rome, c. August 59] (5) I have no idea what will happen to Bibulus. As things are now, he is very highly thought of; when he had the elections put off until October — not a very popular move in normal circumstances — Caesar thought he could talk the people into attacking him, but for all his inflammatory rhetoric, he couldn't get a voice in support. So you see: they are beginning to feel that they have lost the backing of all parties. That brings the prospect of violence closer.

46.

APPIAN *B.C.* 2.14 (50) Caesar realized that he was likely to be away from Rome for a considerable time and that the greater the honours conferred on him, the more envy he would face. As he was afraid that even Pompey, for all his friendship, might become jealous of his great success, he gave him in marriage his daughter Julia, although she was betrothed to Caepio. He also put his most uncompromising partisans into office for the following year. (51) As consuls he designated his friend Aulus Gabinius, and Lucius [Calpurnius] Piso whose daughter he himself married. This made Cato exclaim that high office was being sold out to the highest bidder in the marriage market. (52) As tribunes he chose Vatinius and Clodius Pulcher.

Vatinius was in fact tribune in 59 (see nos. **71** ff.).

47.

CICERO *ad. Q.f.* 1.2 [Rome, c. Nov. 59, to his brother Quintus who was then governor of Asia] (15) Now for the news you really want to hear. We have properly lost our grip on the Republic; so much so that Gaius Cato, a naïve young man but still a Roman citizen and a Cato, barely escaped with his life when he mounted the speaker's platform and called Pompey an 'unofficial dictator'. He had been trying to bring Gabinius to trial for bribery, but the praetors for days on end had made it impossible for anyone to get near them. . . . (16) . . . This is how things stand: if Clodius gives notice of an action against me, the whole of Italy will rush to my support and I shall emerge with my reputation enhanced. If he tries to settle things by violent means, I am confident that with the backing of friend and foe alike we can respond with violence. . . . Any whose sympathies were alienated or lukewarm before have now sided with the 'good' men out of hatred for the tyrants. Pompey and Caesar both make extravagant promises, but I don't trust them enough to relax my preparations. The tribunes designate are friends of ours; the consuls elect have made a very good showing. Next year's praetors are also friendly and vigorous. . . . So keep your spirits up and your hopes high.

Cicero's confident assertions prove in fact to be wildly misguided (see nos. **51** ff.). How did he come to be so deceived?

THE FIRST COUNTER-ATTACKS

Caesar had probably expected the attacks that were made upon his administration as soon as he was out of office and did not leave the vicinity of Rome until he had seen his appointed successors, and especially the tribunes, effectively retaliating.

48.

SUETONIUS *Div. Jul.* 23 (1) When Caesar's consulship was over, the praetors Gaius Memmius and Lucius Domitius proposed an inquiry into his acts of the previous year. Caesar put the matter into the hands of the Senate, but when they would not take it up, and three days had been spent in unprofitable wrangling, he left for his province. At once his quaestor was summoned to face several charges as a preliminary to his own trial. Then he too was arraigned by the tribune Lucius Antistius; but by appealing to the whole College of Tribunes he managed to avoid standing trial, on the ground that he was away on business of national importance.

> The year of office ended on Dec. 10th. Caesar's 'leaving for his province' simply meant that he went outside the precinct of the city, where he could still keep an eye on things. The College of Tribunes comprised the ten tribunes of the year.

Cicero's retrospective view of the last three weeks of 59:

49.

CICERO *Sest.* 40 At the time they were panic-stricken because they thought that all their arrangements and legislation of the previous year were being undermined by the praetors and invalidated by the Senators and leading citizens.

Schol. Bob. on *Sest.* 40. Cicero is talking about the measures which Caesar passed in his consulship, without auspices it appears. The praetors Memmius and Domitius had made moves against him in the Senate and there are extant speeches of Caesar himself in which he attacks them and defends his own conduct. So the reason attributed to Caesar for his seeming connivance at the ruin of Cicero by the tribune Clodius and the consuls Piso and Gabinius was his desire to see that the legislation of his consulship should stand.

> These speeches of Caesar have not survived.

50.

DIO 38.12 (3) When Bibulus came into the forum at the end of his year of office for the ceremonial oath-taking, he was intending to make a speech about the present situation, but Clodius silenced him and then went on to make an attack on Cicero . . . (5) Cicero alienated many people by his speeches and attracted less support

from those he helped than hostility from those he had injured . . .
(7) Besides, he was an incomparable boaster and regarded no man
as his equal; in his speeches and in his daily life he despised everyone and reckoned himself a cut above anyone else. He was a burden
and a trial to others, and even those who shared his sympathies
felt a jealous dislike of him. 13 (1) This led Clodius to hope that he
could soon deal with him if he first paved the way by winning over
the Senate, Knights, and people. His first move was to arrange for
handing out free corn: now that Gabinius and Piso were consuls,
he brought in a bill for distributing it to the needy. (2) He then
restored the societies, called *collegia* in Rome, which had existed
in ancient times but had been disbanded some years ago . . . (6) He
also introduced a bill that none of the magistrates should 'observe
the signs from heaven' on days when the people had to vote on
anything [cf. Cic. *Pis.* 9].

> Compare this picture of Cicero with the confident self-appraisal in no.
> 47. Which may be reckoned the more realistic?

THE EXILE OF CICERO

The opposition to Caesar could be most effectively neutralized by
removing its leading spokesmen. Cicero had resisted all offers of co-
operation; he was a fervent critic of the Caesarian regime and had enough
prestige in senatorial circles to be a real danger. Fortunately his handling
of the Catilinarian executions and the grudge borne against him by
Clodius provided both an excuse for, and a willing executant of, his
banishment. Caesar himself stayed in the background and, as Cicero cast
almost indiscriminate blame on all the friends who, to his horrified
surprise, mutely abandoned him, it was not easy to tell just who was
responsible for his exile.

51.

VELLEIUS 2.45 (1) Publius Clodius, a man of high birth, eloquence
and audacity, who recognized no limits to his powers of speech
or action except his own caprice; a vigorous executant of his own
evil schemes, with a scandalous reputation for having seduced his
own sister and a charge against him for having adulterated and
profaned the most sacred of Roman religious festivals, carried on
a campaign of hatred against Cicero — and what love could there

be between people so dissimilar? He had himself transferred from the patricians to the plebs and during his year as tribune brought in a bill that anyone who had executed a Roman citizen without trial should be forbidden fire and water [i.e. outlawed]; although Cicero was not specifically named in the wording, it was against him alone that the bill was directed. (2) And so this man who had served the state so well found himself tragically exiled as a reward for having saved his country. There was more than a hint that Caesar and Pompey were responsible; it looks as though Cicero brought their crushing weight upon himself by refusing a place on the Commission of Twenty which was responsible for dividing the Campanian land [cf. nos. **30–1**].

The charge against Cicero sprang from his conduct as consul in Dec. 63 when he had had a number of the Catilinarian conspirators executed with senatorial consent, but without trial. He justified his conduct by claiming that it was within the terms of the 'Ultimate Decree' of the Senate which had been issued to deal with the emergency (cf. nos. **294, 399**).

52.

DIO 38.14 (1) Cicero realized what was going on and put up the tribune Lucius Ninnius Quadratus in opposition; Clodius was afraid that this might result in disruptions and delays, and so resorted to deceit. (2) He got Cicero to agree not to stand in the way of his proposals, provided that no charge was brought against him. So Clodius had his proposals passed without a word from Cicero or Ninnius and then launched his attack on Cicero himself. . . . (7) Cicero discarded his senatorial robes and went about dressed as a Knight, calling night and day on all those who had any influence, not only among his friends but among his opponents too; he made his addresses particularly to Pompey and even Caesar whose enmity towards him was still concealed . . . 15 (5) He had no previous suspicion of Pompey and was quite confident of being rescued by him . . . (6) He also expected to have the support of Gabinius, on the grounds of friendship, and Piso, because of his sense of fair play and his kinship with Caesar . . . 16 (5) Piso had seemed to be sympathetic to Cicero and, when he saw that there was no other way out, advised him to leave before there was trouble. This only made Cicero angry; (6) so, as soon as his health

allowed him, Piso appeared in the Assembly and, when asked by
Clodius what he thought of the proposal, replied 'I have no liking
for cruel or sulky behaviour.' When Gabinius was asked the same
thing, he said nothing on Cicero's behalf, and even castigated the
Senate and Knights. 17(1) Caesar had already taken up his command and so, to get his opinion of the measures, Clodius called a
meeting of the Assembly outside the walls. Caesar's pronounce-
ment was that he condemned the illegality of what had been done
in Lentulus' case, (2) but did not approve of the punishment proposed for it . . . (3) Crassus made a show of assisting Cicero through
his son but gave his personal support to the people. Pompey continued to promise assistance but, with a variety of different excuses
at different times, managed to be away from Rome repeatedly and
avoided helping at all. (4) Seeing how things were, Cicero became
alarmed and openly abused everyone including Pompey. He even
made as if to take up arms again, but was prevented by Cato and
Hortensius in case a civil war should result.

> Lentulus was one of the Catilinarian conspirators executed in 63.
> Caesar, in the Senate at the time, had spoken strongly against the death
> penalty which Cicero and later Cato advocated.

Cicero's version of the events:

53.
CICERO *Sest.* 41. Crassus said that my cause ought to be taken up
by the consuls; Pompey also begged for their allegiance, saying
that, as a private citizen, he would support any official cause taken
up by them. But for all his zeal on my behalf, for all his anxiety to
preserve the Republic, he was warned to be more careful by a
number of people purposely planted in my house. They said that I
was plotting against his life in my own home, and nourished the
suspicion by sending letters, messages and personal warnings. He
certainly had nothing to fear from me, but felt that he ought to be
on his guard against them, in case anything was contrived in my
name. Caesar himself, whom some misguided people thought to be
particularly angry with me, was at the gates of the city, in possession of his command; his army was still in Italy and in that army
he had given a post to the brother of my enemy the tribune.

54.

CICERO *Pis.* 77. A large number of distinguished men came to call on Pompey at his Alban home to beg him not to desert my cause which was so closely linked with the safety of the state. He sent them on to you [Piso] and your colleague, asking you to take up the public cause and bring the matter before the Senate; he said that he himself was unwilling to challenge an armed tribune, unless supported by an official resolution, but he would take up arms if they undertook the defence of the state by senatorial decree. [This was Piso's reply:] 78. Cicero could serve the state a second time by giving way. If he resisted, there would be unlimited bloodshed. Finally, neither he himself nor his son-in-law [Caesar] would fail the tribune of the people.

A later version of Pompey's excuse for not helping:

55.

CICERO *ad Att.* 10.4 [Arcanum, April 49] (3) When I was prostrated at his feet, he did not even give me a helping hand, but said he could do nothing against Caesar's wishes.

In Plutarch's account Cicero came to ask in person for Pompey's help, but Pompey slipped out of the back door (Plut. *Cic.* 31). So in the end Cicero accepted the consuls' advice to give way; later, in the speech *pro Sestio* (42 ff.), he set out elaborate reasons why he did not stay and fight. But could he in fact have put up any sort of resistance once his influential friends had deserted him? He was of course bitterly resentful of the treatment he received and perhaps, as Velleius says (no. **51**), he was justified; but against whom should this resentment have been directed — Clodius, the consuls, Pompey or Caesar?

THE REMOVAL OF CATO

Cato was no less of a danger: he had fought Caesar at every step and commanded a significant body of support in spite of his archaic moral posturing. The fact that he was removed to Cyprus at the same time suggests deep-laid intrigue, but the sources offer a wide variety of reasons underlying his mission. Again there is some doubt about the part played by Caesar himself in the affair, but in any case Cato was not under sentence in the same way as Cicero and could perhaps have refused the mission if he had felt it to be a piece of political trickery.

56.

VELLEIUS 2.45 (4) In the course of his tribunate Clodius also removed Marcus Cato from the state under the pretence of giving him a highly honourable mission; he proposed a law that Cato be sent to Cyprus as a quaestor, but with praetorian authority and a quaestor on his staff, to remove Ptolemy from his throne.

> This Ptolemy was the brother of the Egyptian king whose title had just been recognized in Rome (cf. no. **27** n. with Suet. *Div. Jul.* 54.3, Dio 39.21.1).

57.

PLUTARCH *Cat. Min.* 34 (2) So long as Cato was in Rome, Clodius could not hope to achieve his main purpose, which was the over-throw of Cicero. When he entered office therefore, he sent for Cato and put this proposal before him; he said that he regarded Cato as having the greatest integrity of any man in Rome and was pre-pared to put his judgment to the test by giving him the commission to the court of Ptolemy in Cyprus, even though there were many other claimants asking to be sent; but Cato was the only man worthy of it, and he was glad to be able to bestow this favour on him. (3) Cato loudly declared that this was an insult and a trap, not a favour at all. To this Clodius replied with a contemptuous sneer 'Well, if it isn't a favour, you can still make the voyage as a penance', and immediately put the bill for sending out Cato in front of the people, who ratified it. Besides, to go with Cato, he provided no ship, no army and no staff apart from two clerks of whom one was a thief and a scoundrel, the other a dependent of his own. (4) Then, as if the mission to Ptolemy in Cyprus was a trivial one, he also gave him instructions to restore the Byzantine exiles. His intention was to try and keep Cato out of the way for as long as possible while he himself was in office.

58.

CICERO *Sest.* 56. Condemned exiles were restored to Byzantium at the very time when citizens were being driven uncondemned from the state.

Schol. Bob. on *Sest.* 56. Clodius had restored these exiles by his law even though they had been quite legally condemned. This aroused Cicero's anger because he had been thrown into exile uncondemned, while they, who had been properly condemned, were restored.

Could Cicero realistically claim to be 'uncondemned'? See no. **51**.

59.

FLORUS 1.44 (3) The Cypriots were a people who had once con-quered whole nations and given away kingdoms. The island had a reputation for wealth which was entirely justified; but this led the tribune Clodius to order that the king's goods be confiscated even though he was still alive and an ally of Rome.

60.

AMMIANUS 14.8 (15) I don't mind saying that the Roman in-vasion of Cyprus was prompted more by greed than justice; for King Ptolemy was an ally joined to Rome by a treaty, and through no fault of his own had his goods confiscated to replenish the failing Roman treasury.

61.

STRABO 14.6 (6) The main reason for the ruin of King Ptolemy was Publius Clodius Pulcher. In the days when the Cilician pirates were at the height of their power, he had fallen into their hands and sent a messenger to the king asking him to send the ransom money necessary for his release. The king obliged, but with so paltry a sum that the pirates refused to accept it and sent it back in disgust. Even so they released Clodius without a ransom. When he arrived safely home, he remembered the services rendered by both parties and, on becoming tribune, had sufficient influence to see that Marcus Cato was sent to take away Cyprus from its possessor.

62.

CICERO *Sest.* 59. The poor king of Cyprus had always been our friend and ally, and neither the Roman Senate nor commanders had ever entertained any serious suspicions of him. But now, while he was still 'alive and kicking', his goods and chattels were put up for auction in front of his eyes. I tell you, other kings had better look to the security of their thrones with the example of that disastrous year in front of them, when they could see some tribune or other with hundreds of strong-arm men robbing them of their present and prospective power. 60. In doing so, their intention was not to honour Marcus Cato, but to banish him, not to give him a mission to fulfil, but to impose one on him. They declared openly in the Assembly that they had torn out Cato's tongue, which had been so free in its denunciations of extraordinary commissions. [Cicero then explains why Cato had no option but to take up his commission . . .] 63. Here was a man who in the year before [59] had given up going to the Senate, even though he would have found in me a sympathizer for his political ideas, had he been there. Could he now stand there and see me banished, knowing that this sentence amounted to a condemnation of his vote and of the whole Senate [sc. for having supported the proposal to execute the Catilinarian conspirators]?

63.

DIO 38.22 (3) When Ptolemy heard of this decree, he had not the courage to resist the Romans or the fortitude to live on, deprived of his kingdom; so he took poison and killed himself.

Although Cicero blamed Clodius for Cato's removal, he reveals this evidence incriminating Caesar:

64.

CICERO *Dom.* 22. At a public meeting you [Clodius] read a letter which you said had been sent to you by Caesar. . . . He congratulated you, so you said, on ridding your tribunate of Marcus Cato and depriving him of further opportunities for speaking about extraordinary commands. Caesar never sent you such a letter — or if he did he had no desire for it to be read out at a public meeting. In any case, whether he did send it or whether you just invented it, by reading it out you made clear your intentions of discrediting Cato.

Caesar's political arrangements for the future at Rome depended on his ties with Pompey and Crassus (now reinforced by marriage), the election of sympathetic consuls, the installation of Clodius as tribune, and the removal of Cicero and Cato. This might have been expected to give him thorough protection but it could not be fully relied upon. What were the limitations? On the other hand, why was not the opposition brought against Caesar immediately after his year of office (nos. 48–9) more effective?

II. Caesar's Provincial Command

The tenure of the consulship was no longer, as it had been in earlier Republican days, the summit of political ambition. The power that it enabled a man to wield during office was limited and the prestige of having held the office was diminished. Even Caesar, for all his disregard of the constitutional safeguards, had not achieved any permanent domination and was vulnerable to attack the moment he left office. Where was he to look now? The lesson of the last four decades had been that prestige was most easily won on foreign battlefields. Provincial commands were often prolonged beyond the statutory year, and a sequence of successful campaigns against a wealthy enemy could guarantee the general not only a personal fortune, but also the solid backing of his army. Since the reforms of Marius in 104, the army had become a body of professional soldiers, looking to the spoils of war for their livelihood and owing far more loyalty to their commander than to their country of birth. This devotion could be exploited to endanger the Roman state, as it had been by Sulla in 88, and by Pompey in 78. It was therefore essential for Caesar, if he was to compete with his political rivals and capitalize on the achievements of his consulship, that he should acquire a provincial command which would give him the same scope as both of them had enjoyed. This chapter presents some of the alternatives open to him and suggests reasons why he chose as he did.

A. The choice of provinces

GAUL AND ILLYRIA

If, as seems most likely, Caesar's choice of province was primarily determined by his desire for campaigns which would bring him prestige and financial profit, the field was limited. Asia had been exhausted by the fighting, continuous since 87 and recently rounded off in triumph by Pompey; Spain had been fought over for even longer and Caesar's personal acquaintance with the country in 61–60 probably convinced him that nothing spectacular could still be achieved there. The current trouble spots were, it seems, in Gaul and the Balkans; both, providentially, were available. Metellus Celer, appointed governor of Transalpine Gaul in

March 60, seems to have been later deprived of his command and in any case died at the beginning of the following year. In the East, Caesar could avail himself of the province of Illyria, which did not usually have a separate governor but was amalgamated with Macedonia. Its advantage over Macedonia was that, like Transalpine Gaul, it was contiguous with Italy.

The potential danger in Gaul:

65.

CICERO *ad Att.* 1.19 [15 March 60] (2) And now there is a national alarm current about the possibility of war in Gaul. Our 'brothers' the Aedui have recently suffered defeat and there is little doubt that the Helvetii are in arms and making raids on the Province. The Senate has passed a resolution that the provinces of Gaul be allotted to the consuls, that levies be held and exemptions suspended, and that a diplomatic mission be sent round the Gallic states to try and persuade them not to join forces with the Helvetii.

> For the defeat of the Aedui and the incursions of the Helvetii, see nos. **97, 100.**

> 'The Province' was the area in S.E. France (retaining the name as 'Provence' nowadays) which up till then marked the limit of the Roman occupation of Gaul.

On the strength of this news, the consul Q. Caecilius Metellus was made governor of Transalpine Gaul for the year 59.

66.

CICERO *ad Att.* 1.20 [Rome, May 60] (5) Your Metellus is an excellent consul; my only reservation is that he is none too pleased at the news of peace in Gaul. He's after a triumph, I suppose.

In June 60, the consul Metellus firmly opposed the land-bill introduced by Flavius on behalf of Pompey's veterans.

67.

DIO 37.50 (4) Metellus did not give way even when Flavius threatened not to let him go to his allotted province unless he agreed to allow the passage of the bill; on the contrary he continued to stay in the city quite happily [cf. no. **8** n].

The fact that Metellus continued to stay in the city suggests that he *was* deprived of his provincial command. The contrary evidence in no. **68** below might be taken to refer to Celer's tenure of the proconsulship of Cisalpine Gaul in 62.

68.

PLINY *N.H.* 2 (170) According to Nepos, Metellus Celer, (who was Afranius' colleague in the consulship) received, when proconsul in Gaul, some Indians as a present from the king of the Suebians; they had been making a trading voyage from India when storms had swept them off course to Germany.

Metellus probably died in the first half of the year 59, after resolute opposition to the passing of Caesar's first agrarian law. (Dio. 38.7.1, Cic. *Cael.* 59).

The province of Macedonia had been governed by C. Octavius, father of the Emperor Augustus (*I.L.S.* 47).

69.

SUETONIUS *Aug.* 3 (2) He governed his province with as much justice as courage: not only did he defeat the Bessi and Thracians in a major campaign, but he treated the allies so well that Marcus Cicero, in a letter which is still extant [*ad Q.f.* 1.1.21, written in late 60], advised and encouraged his brother Quintus, at that time making himself unpopular with a proconsular command in Asia, to copy his neighbour Octavius' methods for winning the goodwill of the allies. 4 (1) On his way back from Macedonia he died suddenly before he could put himself forward as a candidate for the consulship.

There appears also to have been a governor of Illyria in 59 although the date is conjectural.

70.

CICERO *ad Fam.* 13.42 [Rome, ?59] (1) Lucius Lucceius, one of my very dearest friends, has asked me to send you unlimited thanks. He says you have been most liberal and extravagant in all your promises to his tax-collectors. . . . All the people of Bullio have made it clear that they will repay Lucceius as Pompey wishes.

The letter is addressed 'to the proconsul Lucius Culleolus', and the reference to the town of Bullio makes it seem likely that his province was Illyria.

THE LAW OF VATINIUS

Under the existing law (the *Lex Sempronia*) the Senate assigned provinces to consuls before their year of office began, or as much as eighteen months before they could actually go to the province concerned. According to Suetonius, token provinces were assigned in this way to the consuls of 59. Even if this was the case, Caesar paid no attention and the bill of Vatinius for giving him command of Cisalpine Gaul and Illyria gave rise to Cicero's complaint that he had 'deprived the Senate of the right to assign provinces' (Cic. *Vat.* 36). The province of Transalpine Gaul was added later on senatorial authority.

71.

SUETONIUS *Div. Jul.* 19 (2) The *optimates* took care to see that for the consuls of the next year [59] the most undemanding provinces should be allotted, that is 'the woods and pastures'.

> It is not known what was entailed in this command, but it clearly cannot have been anything important.

72.

SUETONIUS *Div. Jul.* 22 (1) So, with the backing of his father-in-law and son-in-law [Piso and Pompey], Caesar chose out of all the many provinces available the Gauls as being the most likely to provide him with riches and opportunities for triumphs. To begin with, it is true, he received Cisalpine Gaul with Illyria as well, by the law of Vatinius; but soon the Senate gave him Further Gaul as well, as they were afraid that the people would give him that too if they themselves refused.

73.

DIO 38.8 (5) The populace gave him the command in Illyria and Cisalpine Gaul with three legions for five years, and the Senate assigned him Transalpine Gaul with another legion.

74.

APPIAN *B.C.* 2.13 (49) Caesar put on shows and circuses which

were more lavish and splendid and extravagant than any previous
spectacles. They were well beyond his means and he had to borrow
on all sides; but as a result he was given the command in both
Cisalpine and Transalpine Gaul for five years, with four legions
under his control.

> This is substantially the same account as in Plut. *Cat. Min.* 33.

Suetonius is the only source which suggests that the Senate tried to
prevent Caesar getting a worthwhile province. We should probably
accept the information, as it helps to explain why Caesar relied upon
Vatinius and the people to give him his initial command. But why then
did the Senate subsequently offer him Transalpine Gaul as well? Is the
reason given in no. **72** adequate? For further information about the
situation in that part of Gaul, see Section D.

B. Cisalpine Gaul

The Po valley was even in those days rich in natural resources and man-
power, and Caesar used his Cisalpine province as his main recruiting
centre. It was however no less important as affording direct communi-
cation with Rome and he returned there almost every winter. His founding
of the colony of Novum Comum gave him personal connections with the
area which he later exploited in campaigning for political support.

75.

STRABO 5.1 [From the section on Cisalpine Gaul] (12) The arable
land produces crops of many different kinds and the forests are so
rich in acorns that Rome is largely fed on the herds of pigs that
come from there. Because the land is well-watered the millet crop
is particularly good; this is the best safeguard against famine as it
can stand any kind of weather and can never fail even if there is a
shortage of every other cereal. There are also wonderful pitch-
works, and the abundance of wine is indicated by the size of the
wooden storage jars which are bigger than houses.

76.

APPIAN *B.C.* 2.26 (98) Caesar founded the city of Novum Comum
at the foot of the Alps and gave it Latin rights [etc. as in no. **333**].

> For other references to the colony, see Strabo 5.1.6, Ascon. *in Pison.* 2–3
> and no. **334** which dates the foundation to 59.

North Italy was Caesar's initial source of recruits (*B.G.* 1.10.3) and he made frequent use of the area for collecting reinforcements thereafter: two legions in 57 (*B.G.* 2.2.1), one in 54 (*B.G.* 5.24.4), three in 53 (*B.G.* 6.1), and a general levy in 52 (*B.G.* 7.1.1). Even if he was not recruiting he liked to make annual visits at the end of the campaigning season, as in 58/7 (*B.G.* 2.2.1), 57/6 (*B.G.* 2.35.3), 56/5 (*B.G.* 4.6.3), 55/4 (*B.G.* 5.1.1), 53/2 (*B.G.* 6.44.3), 51/0 (*B.G.* 8.50–51). Everyone knew that the purpose of these visits was as much political as administrative.

77.

PLUTARCH *Caes.* 20 (2) There he established himself [in Cisalpine Gaul in winter 58/7] and carried on his campaign for political support. Many people came to see him and he satisfied all their demands, sending them away already better off, or at any rate with the expectation of being so. In fact, throughout the time of his Gallic command, he was, without Pompey realizing it, either using the weapons of Roman citizens to defeat the enemy, or using the money taken from the enemy to win the submission of the citizens.

C. Illyria

THE NATURE OF THE PROVINCE

The province of Illyria incorporated little more than the strip of Dalmatian coast captured at the end of the third century and spasmodically patrolled thereafter so as to discourage piracy. The hinterland was not conquered until the time of Augustus. The country as a whole was extremely poor, but because of its proximity to Italy was sometimes treated as a training area for Roman arms.

78.

APPIAN *Ill.* 1 The Greeks reckon as Illyrians the people who live north of Macedon and Thrace, from Chaonia and Thesprotia to the Danube. That is the length of the country; in breadth it extends from the borders of Macedon and Thrace to Pannonia, the Adriatic and the foothills of the Alps.

79.

AUGUSTUS *Res Gest.* 30 The Pannonian peoples, whom no Roman army had ever reached before my Principate, were defeated [in 12–9 B.C.] by Tiberius Nero, then my stepson and legate; I brought them under the sway of the Roman people and extended the frontiers of Illyria to the bank of the river Danube.

A description of some of the Illyrian tribes:

80.

STRABO 7.5 (4) The Iapodes: their country is wretchedly poor and the staple diet is spelt and millet. . . . (5) It is a peculiarity of the Dalmatians that they divide up their lands every eight years; they do not use money either, which is unusual for a coastal tribe, but common among barbarians generally. . . . (6) The Ardaei were driven inland by the Romans from the sea which their piracy had made unsafe and were compelled to take up farming. As the country is poor and rugged and quite unsuitable for farming, the tribe was completely ruined and very nearly lost altogether. Other peoples in the area suffered the same fate. . . . (7) The Dardani are an un-civilized people, living in caves which they dig underneath their manure heaps; but they are fond of music and devote a lot of time to playing on wind- and string-instruments.

81.

FLORUS 1.19 (2) At intervals the Ligurians, the Insubrian Gauls and indeed the Illyrians would cause trouble. . . . (3) It was as if a god was always driving them on to it to ensure that Roman arms would not rot away from rust and mildew. These everyday, almost domestic, enemies blooded the new recruits, and the Romans could sharpen the edge of their valour on either people, just like a sword on a whetstone.

BUREBISTAS

The province of Illyria by itself could not offer Caesar very much scope and it seems more likely that his reason for taking it was to enable him to come to grips with the expanding empire of the Getae. These people came from the Danube basin and seem to have been spreading their influence westwards at about this time under their king Burebistas. We cannot be sure about the dating as the chronology preserved by Jordanes is unreliable, but circumstantial evidence points to a coincidence of the fortunes of Caesar and Burebistas.

82.

STRABO 7.3 (11) Burebistas the Getan took over the leadership of the tribe and put new spirit into the men who were demoralized by continuous wars. He trained them in sobriety and obedience, and reanimated them so effectively that within a few years he had established a large kingdom and got control of most of the states neighbouring the Getae. Even the Romans were worried, as he did not hesitate to cross the Danube and ravage Thrace as far as Illyria and Macedon; he crushed the Celts who lived among the Thracians and Illyrians, and completely annihilated the Taurisci and the Boii under Cratisirus. (12) The Getan people who had been raised to such power by Burebistas were cut down by civil wars and Roman arms, but still even now [sc. the end of the first century B.C.] they can put 40,000 men into the field. . . . (13) At the time when the numbers of the Dacians and Getans were at their peak, they could produce an army of 200,000.

> This is the only detailed account we have of the achievements of Burebistas. We know that the Augustan historian, Pompeius Trogus, also covered the subject, as a chapter heading from his thirty-second volume refers to his account of 'the expansion of the Dacian empire through their king Burebistas'. However the narrative is lost and it is not included in the works of his excerptor Justin.

83.

JORDANES Get.11. 67. When Buruista was king of the Goths, Decineus came into the country of the Goths at the time when Sulla won the leading position among the Romans. Buruista took up this Decineus and gave him almost kingly power; by his advice the Goths ravaged the lands of the Germans which are now in the hands of the Franks. Caesar in fact, who first of all the Romans won for himself the position of Emperor and subjected almost the whole world to his domination . . . even he, though he made many attempts, could not subjugate the Goths.

84.

DIO CHRYSOSTOM 36.4. The last and most disastrous capture of Borysthenes was about 150 years ago. On that occasion the Getae seized not only Borysthenes but also the other cities on the left shore of the Black Sea, as far as Apollonia.

Borysthenes was at the mouth of the Dnieper; Apollonia about 125 miles west of the Bosporus. This dating would put the capture at about 50 B.C.

85.

S.I.G.[4] 762: (v. 22) Recently when Burebistas was first and greatest of the Thracian kings and had possession of all the land beyond the river [Danube] and on this side of it. . . .

This inscription can be dated a little after 48 B.C. by a reference to Pompey's campaign in north Greece that year.

THE CAMPAIGN PLANNED FOR 45

The situation that developed in Gaul effectively prevented Caesar from undertaking an Illyrian campaign at this time (see next chapter). However when thirteen years later his supremacy was finally established at Rome, he seems to have planned another eastern offensive, which may shed some light on his intentions in 58.

86.

APPIAN *B.C.* 2. 110 (459) And now [in 45] . . . he decided to embark on a long campaign against the Getae and the Parthians. He set his sights against the Getae first, a hard, warlike people on the frontier of Italy. . . . (460) As a preliminary he sent sixteen legions of infantry and ten thousand cavalry across the Adriatic.

87.

APPIAN *Ill.* 13. When everything was settled, Caesar returned to Rome and started preparing for campaigns against the Getae and the Parthians. The Illyrians were afraid that he might attack them as they were on his way and so sent delegates to Rome to ask pardon for what they had done [the destruction of a Caesarian army under Gabinius in 48], and offer friendship and alliance.

88.

VELLEIUS 2.59 (4) When the civil wars were over . . . he sent Octavian to Apollonia to study, intending in time to have him on his staff against the Getae and later the Parthians.

89.

SUETONIUS *Div. Jul.* 44 (3) [Among the projects cut short by Caesar's death were . . .] To check the Dacians who had poured into Pontus and Thrace, and then to embark on a war against the Parthians by way of Lesser Armenia.

90.

STRABO 7.3 (5) And when the king of the Getae was Burebistas, against whom the deified Caesar was preparing to launch a campaign, Decineus fulfilled the post of priest-councillor. . . . (12) Burebistas was overthrown by an insurrection before the Romans could send an expedition against him; and those who succeeded to his kingdom divided it up into several parts.

> If this account is accurate, it suggests that Caesar's plans for a campaign against the Getae were cut short by Burebistas' death, not his own.

The evidence that Caesar seriously intended to launch a Balkan campaign in 58 is admittedly incomplete. There is no mention of such an idea in the contemporary writings of Cicero or Caesar himself, nor in our main secondary sources, Appian, Plutarch, and Dio. But is that sufficient reason for discounting the possibility? Is there any other way of explaining why Caesar chose the province of Illyria before he was assigned Transalpine Gaul?

D. Transalpine Gaul

THE ALLOBROGES

The most persistent trouble makers of recent years in the Transalpine province had been the Allobroges, who occupied the area between the Rhône and the Isère. They had been involved, either by accident or design, in the conspiracy of Catiline in 63 and had then been subjected to a series of retaliatory campaigns under the governor C. Pomptinus in 62–59.

91.

CICERO *Prov. Cos.* 32. Not long ago that gallant gentleman, Gaius Pomptinus, who shared my difficulties, dangers and deliberations, broke up by his campaigns the war of the Allobroges which suddenly burst out under the impetus of that criminal conspiracy.

He defeated the aggressors and was content to rest on his laurels after freeing the state from fear.

For Pomptinus' part in unmasking the Allobroges' conspiracy in 63, when he was praetor, see Cic. *Cat.* 3.5.14; Cic. *Flacc.* 102. For an account of his campaign against the Allobroges in 62–59, see Dio 37. 47–9.

Cicero held it against Vatinius that he objected to some public thanksgivings in 59; the Scholiast says that these thanksgivings were in honour of Pomptinus:

92.

SCHOL. BOB. on Cic. *Vat.* 30. Gaius Pomptinus was trying to get a triumph for his successful achievements in Gaul, but was unable to do so because of the opposition raised by Caesar's friends who were keen to see that all the credit for peace and victory should go to no one else but Caesar.

According to Caesar, the Allobroges were still not regarded as being very friendly to Rome and the Helvetii thought it would be easy to get a passage through their land as they migrated westwards (cf. nos. **100** f., **105** ff.)

93.

CAESAR *B.G.* 1.6 (2) Between the territory of the Helvetii and the Allobroges, who had recently been pacified, flows the Rhine, which can be forded at a number of places. (3) The last town of the Allobroges, which is nearest to Helvetian territory, is Geneva. From there a bridge connects with the Helvetii. The Allobroges still did not appear to be very favourably disposed towards the Roman people and the Helvetii thought they could easily be persuaded, or if need be compelled, to let them have a passage through their country.

THE AEDUI

Roman interests in Gaul extended outside the boundaries of their Transalpine province. Among the beneficiaries of their patronage were the Aedui who lived to the north. They were now in danger of being submerged by a Gallic coalition headed by the Sequani and assisted by the German king Ariovistus [cf. nos. **97, 121** ff.]. The need to defend them against this threat could be used to justify Caesar's intervention.

94.

CAESAR *B.G.* 1.35 (4) In the year when Marcus [Valerius] Messalla and Marcus [Pupius] Piso were consuls [61] the Senate had passed a resolution to the effect that any governor of the Roman province in Gaul should protect the Aedui and the other friends of the Roman people, so far as the public interest would allow.

95.

CAESAR *B.G.* 6.12 (1) When Caesar arrived in Gaul, he found two factions, one led by the Aedui, the other by the Sequani. (2) The Aedui had traditionally been the stronger power, and they had large numbers of dependants. The Sequani, to make up for their comparative weakness, had attached themselves to Ariovistus and the Germans, whom they brought in at the cost of considerable sacrifices and promises. (3) After a number of successful battles and the destruction of all the Aeduan nobility, they had reached such a position of superiority that they attracted onto their side most of the Aeduan dependants. (4) They took the sons of their chiefs as hostages and made them swear in public not to plot against the Sequani; they occupied the adjacent territory which they had seized by force, and held the supremacy of all Gaul. (5) It was this crisis which drove Diviciacus to go and beg help from the Senate at Rome. His mission was a failure and he returned.

Diviciacus apparently stayed with Cicero when he was in Rome (Cic. *Div.* 1.90).

After Caesar's victory over the Helvetii in 58 (cf. nos. **105–120**) he listened to a speech from Diviciacus about the Aeduan predicament and decided to open war on the Germans.

96.

CAESAR *B.G.* 1.33 (2) There were many factors leading Caesar to suppose that he would have to take deliberate action; the Aedui, who had often been given the title of 'brothers and kinsmen' by the Senate, were now subject to German domination; their hostages were in the hands of Ariovistus and the Sequani. This, he considered, was a gross insult to himself and the state, in view of the greatness of the Roman Empire. (3) The Germans were getting used to the idea of crossing the Rhine, and the massive influx into Gaul posed a danger to the Roman state; (4) they were a wild, uncivilized people who, he thought, would hardly refrain from doing as the Cimbri and Teutones had done; once they had occupied Gaul they would move in on the Province and from there march against Italy. These developments would have to be countered with decisive action.

> The Cimbri and Teutones defeated a number of Roman armies in the course of their migrations westwards in 113–105, but were later destroyed by Marius. (cf. nos. **121** f.)

ARIOVISTUS

The danger to the Aedui was not simply a matter of losing tribal supremacy: the number of Germans whom Ariovistus brought into the country constituted a potential danger to the whole of Gaul. Caesar however does not seem to have treated it as a threat to begin with, and even went out of his way to extend to him the official friendship of Rome. This may, of course, just have been a subterfuge by Caesar to buy Ariovistus' co-operation until such time as he was ready to deal with him (cf. nos. **121–131**).

97.
(From Diviciacus' speech.)
CAESAR *B.G.* 1.31 (3) 'In Gaul as a whole there are two factions — one is led by the Aedui, the other by the Arverni. (4) After a protracted struggle for supremacy between the two sides, the Arverni and Sequani tried to hire assistance from Germany. (5) At first the Germans sent about 15,000 men across the Rhine, but later more of these wild savages came over, attracted by the rich lands and crops of the Gauls; now there are anything up to 120,000 of them in Gaul. (6) We, the Aedui, and our dependants fought against them time and again, but we were defeated disastrously and lost our Senate, our Knights and our leading citizens. (7) Once

we were the greatest power in Gaul, thanks to our own spirit and the friendship and co-operation of the Roman people; but now we are so ruined by disastrous battles that we have been compelled to surrender the noblest men in the state as hostages to the Sequani and bind the state under an oath not to try and get the hostages back, or beg assistance from the Roman people, or do anything to escape being under the dominion and sway of the Sequani. (8) I am the only Aeduan in the whole state who could not be brought to swear or give my children as hostages. (9) That was why I fled from the state and came to Rome to ask the Senate for help as only I was not held by oath or hostages. (10) But things have turned out worse for the victorious Sequani than for the defeated Aedui; the German king Ariovistus has settled in their land and annexed a third of their territory, the best throughout Gaul. Now he has ordered the Sequani to cede him another area of the same size to accommodate the 23,000 Harudes who joined him a few months afterwards. (11) In a year or two all the lands of Gaul will have to be evacuated and all the Germans will come across the Rhine, as there is no comparison between Gallic and German farming-land or standard of living. (12) Ariovistus defeated the Gallic armies at Magetobriga and has proved himself a cruel and arrogant overlord. He has demanded the children of leading families as hostages and treated them with great brutality as a warning against opposition to his will or inclination in anything. (13) He is a vicious, reckless savage and his rule is quite intolerable. (14) If you, Caesar, and the Roman people do not do something, the Gauls will all be compelled to follow the same course as the Helvetii: to leave their homes and look for somewhere else to settle and live, away from the Germans.'

Later when Caesar came face to face with Ariovistus, he reminded him of his obligations to Rome:

98.

CAESAR B.G. 1.43 (4) 'The Senate gave you the title "King and Friend" and was very generous in sending you presents. Few have had this privilege, and usually in return for exceptional services. (5) You had no proper cause for approaching the Senate or making this request, but still obtained the favour you wanted, thanks to the kindness and generosity of myself and the Senate.'

It was certainly strange that Ariovistus should have received presents as well as his honorific title from the Senate. It was more usual to have to pay for such a privilege. In fact Cicero said of this year, 59: 'What king did not expect to have to buy what he did not possess, or buy back what once belonged to him?' (Cic. *Sest.* 66). Later writers ascribe to Caesar personal responsibility for giving Ariovistus this honour (see no. **131** with Appian *Celt.* 16).

THE HELVETII

The activities of the Helvetii had given rise to concern since at any rate the year 60 (see no. **65**), although there is no means of telling whether the threatened migrations represented a genuine social need, as Caesar suggests, or were merely a front for Orgetorix' dynastic ambitions. Caesar would naturally support the first alternative as explaining why the Helvetii persisted in their plans for migration even after Orgetorix was dead (cf. no. **105**).

99.
(From the introduction to the first book of the *B.G.*)
CAESAR *B.G.* 1.1 (4) The Helvetii are also more redoubtable than other Gauls because they engage in almost daily battles with the Germans, either carrying war into German territory or trying to keep them out of their own.

> This might help to explain why in 59 Caesar was anxious to remain on friendly terms with Ariovistus and the Germans.

100.
CAESAR *B.G.* 1.2 (1) Much the most prominent and wealthy man among the Helvetii was Orgetorix. In the consulship of Marcus Messalla and Marcus Piso [61], dynastic ambition drove him to form a conspiracy among the nobility. He persuaded the citizens to march out of the country in full force, (2) assuring them that their superior fighting powers would easily win them mastery of Gaul. (3) What made it easy to convince them was that the territory of the Helvetii had strict natural confines: on one side the Rhine, deep and wide, marked the frontier with Germany; on the other the high Jura mountains separated them from the Sequani; and Lake Geneva and the river Rhône were between them and the

Roman Province. (4) That meant that their range of movement and the opportunities for fighting their neighbours were considerably limited, and this was frustrating for a naturally aggressive people. (5) The size of the population, with their military prowess and courage, needed more space than their present area of 240 miles by 180 . . . 3 (2) The people reckoned that two years was long enough to make all the necessary arrangements for migration and pledged themselves by law to move in the third year. (3) Orgetorix was chosen to supervise the arrangements (4) and undertook a mission to other states. In the course of it he persuaded Casticus of the Sequani to usurp the royal position which his father held in the state (his father was Catamantaloedis who had been king of the Sequani for many years and had been given the title 'Friend of the Roman People' by the Senate); (5) he persuaded the Aeduan Dumnorix to make a similar attempt and gave his own daughter for him to marry (Dumnorix was the brother of Diviciacus, who at that time held the highest office in the state, and was particularly popular with the ordinary people). . . . (7) On the strength of Orgetorix' arguments they bound themselves with oaths of common loyalty, hoping that the usurpation of royal power and the combination of three such formidable and resolute tribes would enable them to take over the whole of Gaul.

When the Helvetian people learnt about the conspiracy, they tried to put Orgetorix on trial for treason. He protected himself by collecting an army of retainers, but died shortly afterwards, perhaps at his own hand (*B.G.* 1.4.1–3).

101.

DIO 38.31 (2) The Helvetii were a numerous people and had not enough land for their large population; but they were unwilling to send off part of their citizen body to found a colony in case the separation should make them more vulnerable to attack by people who had a grievance against them; so instead, they decided to migrate in full force in the hope of finding some other larger and better territory in which to settle.

The Helvetii also had a reputation for brigandage in spite of the natural wealth of their country (Strabo 4.3.3).

There can be no doubting the existence of potential trouble-centres in Transalpine Gaul, but it is not easy to see which area in summer 59 demanded such immediate attention that Caesar was prepared to request and the Senate to grant an extension of his province to deal with it: the Allobroges were 'pacified', the Helvetian migration set back by the death of Orgetorix, the Aeduan situation dormant and Ariovistus positively befriended by Caesar. Why is there no mention in the sources of the actual circumstances which prompted Caesar to focus his attention on Transalpine Gaul? Could it be because Caesar had in fact to manufacture a pretext for war?

III. Caesar's Plans for Conquest

Caesar entered his provincial command faced with a choice of three opportunities for intervention in Gaul and the possibility of a major Illyrian campaign. He could undertake to protect the Aedui from the Arverni, and both from Ariovistus; he could also set himself to defend the Gallic province from the potential danger of the Helvetian migration, or the north-east frontier of Italy from the imperial expansion of the Getae. All of these afforded an initial pretext for war, but if we accept the contention of the ancient sources that Caesar was looking for a major field of conquest, we may ask how and why Caesar came to abandon the idea of an eastern campaign, which might have seemed at first the best long-term prospect; and how events in Gaul developed so as to enable him to undertake the conquest of the whole country. It is clearly essential to our assessment of Caesar's statesmanship that we should determine whether the conquest of Gaul was justifiable in terms of Roman foreign policy or whether it was the result of Caesar's personal ambition. The question however is not easily answered as there is hardly any contemporary source material independent of Caesar's own account in the 'Commentaries'. Although it is a matter for dispute how these books were put together in their final form, they were clearly derived from the yearly accounts that Caesar sent back to Rome to justify to the Senate the continuation of his command. It could hardly be expected that they would contain anything which would reflect badly on his conduct of the war: the narrative records his successes and minimizes his failures, and where he concerns himself with motivation there is never a hint of anything discreditable or self-interested. We have to judge Caesar on his own testimony, and the only way in which we can hope to substantiate suspicions about the veracity of his account is by finding inconsistent and implausible details in it. At no point does Caesar himself talk of the prospect or possibility of conquering the whole of Gaul. Each campaign is justified separately, to discount the idea of a preconceived overall strategy. The Roman public however soon accepted the notion that Caesar's ultimate purpose was complete conquest. As early as the summer of 56, when Cicero was persuaded to speak in favour of Caesar retaining his command, he based his argument on the assumption that Caesar had set himself a comprehensive objective which he had not yet fully attained (cf. nos. **183** ff.). Later writers attribute the succession of events to Fortune, but perhaps such a view is intended to invite scepticism rather than acceptance.

102.

CICERO *Prov. Cos.* 32. Gentlemen, under Caesar's leadership, we have fought an offensive against the Gallic people, whereas before we only repelled their attacks. It always used to be the policy of our generals to keep these peoples at bay and avoid aggression. . . . But Caesar's policy has, I observe, been quite different. He was not content with making war on those whom he saw already in arms against the Roman people. No, he wanted the whole of Gaul forced to recognize our sovereignty.

103.

FLORUS 1.45 (1) After Pompey's forces had overrun Asia, Fortune handed over to Caesar all that remained in Europe. (2) To him were left the most formidable people of all, the Gauls and Germans; and even the Britons, whom he had a mind to conquer even though they were on the other side of the world.

104.

DIO 38.31 (1) So much for the events in Rome [during 58]. In Gaul, Caesar found no signs of hostility; everything was absolutely quiet in fact. But the peace did not last; one war after another kept on breaking out spontaneously against him, so that he was able to achieve his greatest ambition by fighting continuously and setting everything to rights.

A. The Gallic campaigns

THE HELVETII

Whatever Caesar's original plans may have been, the news in early 58 that the Helvetii were after all on the move prompted him to action. The campaign gave him his first success, but he is at such pains to justify it that one might think he was deliberately trying to forestall criticism. Perhaps the Helvetii were not such a real threat as he made out.

105.

CAESAR *B.G.* 1.5 (1) Even after the death of Orgetorix the Helvetii did not give up their determination to carry out their intended migration from the country. (2) When they thought that they were ready for the enterprise, they set fire to their towns, twelve in all, as many as four hundred villages and the rest of their private buildings; (3) They burned all their corn except what they intended to take with them so that, with the hope of returning home removed, they would be readier to face every danger. They ordered every man to bring with him from home enough flour to provide food for three months. (4) They persuaded their neighbours the Raurici, Tulingi and Latovici to follow the same plan, burn their towns and villages, and set out with them; and they accepted as partners and allies the Boii who had lived across the Rhine and then crossed into the territory of Noricum and attacked Noreia.

Caesar had some reason for protecting Noreia (which included much of modern Austria); it was very rich in the materials he would need for his campaign — metals, hides, and foodstuffs (Strabo 4.6.12, 5.1.8), whose normal outlet was through the port of Aquileia. Their eastern border was also threatened by the Getae (see no. **82**), and perhaps for that reason they had joined Ariovistus to them by marriage alliance (*B.G.* 1.53.4).

106.

CAESAR *B.G.* 1.7 (1) When Caesar was told that the Helvetii were attempting to make their way through the Roman Province, he hastened his departure from Rome and, making all possible speed, arrived at Geneva. (2) From the whole province he levied as many troops as he could (there being only one legion in the whole of Transalpine Gaul) and ordered the bridge at Geneva to be cut down. (3) When the Helvetii heard of his arrival they sent representatives to him . . . to tell him that their intention was to make their way through the Province without doing any damage, because there was no other way for them to go; and to ask him for his permission to do so. . . . (5) Caesar, to allow time for the soldiers he had levied to assemble, replied that he would take a little while to think it over and told them to return on 13 April if they wanted anything further. [Caesar occupied the interval by fortifying the frontier between the Helvetii and the Roman Province.] . . . 8 (3) When the day came which he had agreed upon with their representatives and they returned, he said that it was not in keeping with the traditional behaviour of the Roman people to allow anyone a passage through the Province; and he made it clear that he would prevent any attempts to use force.

Caesar is more explicit about his motive for the 58 campaign than for any other.

107.

CAESAR *B.G.* 1.7 (4) Caesar did not think that he ought to make concessions to the Helvetii, because he remembered that the consul Lucius Cassius had been killed by the Helvetii, and his army defeated and made to go under the yoke; besides, he did not suppose that men who were inclined to be unfriendly would refrain from damage and mischief if they were given the opportunity of passing through the Province.

cf. no. **93.**

Other references to the defeat of Lucius Cassius in 107 make it appear that he was the aggressor:

108a.

OROSIUS 5.15 (23) Lucius Cassius, the consul in Gaul, pursued the Tigurini to the Ocean, but was surrounded by them in an ambush and killed.

108b.

LIVY *Per.* 65. The consul Lucius Cassius was destroyed with his army by the Gallic Tigurini, a tribe of the Helvetii which had seceded from the state, in the territory of the Nitiobriges in south-west Gaul.

109.

CAESAR *B.G.* 1.9 (1) The only way remaining was through the Sequani; but because of its narrowness they could not use it without the Sequani giving their permission. (2) As they could not get this permission on their own, they sent a request to the Aeduan Dumnorix to act as their spokesman and obtain this favour from the Sequani. (3) Dumnorix, by his favours and liberality, had won

c

great influence among the Sequani and was also friendly with the Helvetii because he had married the daughter of Orgetorix; but he was an ardent revolutionary, inspired by dreams of kingship, and anxious to have as many states as possible bound to him by obligations. (4) So he undertook the mission and obtained leave from the Sequani for the Helvetii to go through their territory; he also arranged for both sides to exchange hostages — the Sequani to guarantee free passage for the Helvetii, the Helvetii to ensure that they would not cause any damage as they passed through.

For Dumnorix cf. no. **100.**

110.

CAESAR *B.G.* 1.10 (1) Caesar was told that the Helvetii intended to make their way through the Sequani and Aedui into the territory of the Santones. This is not far from the land of the Tolosates, whose state is inside the Province. (2) He realized that if this happened the danger to the Province would be very great, with warlike people unfriendly to Rome next to a district which was very rich in corn and unprotected.

The Santones lived on the west coast of Gaul, in the departments of Charente and Gironde; this is in fact about 150 miles north-west of the territory of the Tolosates. What then was the danger to the Province?

111.

CAESAR *B.G.* 1.11 (1) When the Helvetii had brought their troops through the defiles into Sequani territory, they went on to the land of the Aedui and began devastating their fields. (2) The Aedui, unable to defend themselves or their possessions, sent to ask Caesar for help. . . . (4) At the same time the Ambarri, who have family connexions with the Aedui, told Caesar that their fields had been ravaged and that it would not be easy for them to keep so strong an enemy out of their towns. (5) The Allobroges too, who had villages and possessions across the Rhône, fled to Caesar to protest that they had nothing left except their land. (6) Caesar was persuaded by these representations that he should not stand and wait for the Helvetii to reach the land of the Santones after ruining the fortunes of all his allies on the way.

Caesar attacked the Helvetii as they were crossing the Saône in the middle of the night. Three-quarters of them had already got across, but the fourth division consisting of the Tigurini was caught and destroyed.

112.

CAESAR *B.G.* 1.12 (5) The people of this canton, within the memory of the last generation, had left their homes on their own initiative, killed the consul Lucius Cassius and made his army go under the yoke. (6) So, whether by chance or by divine arrangement, the part of Helvetia which had inflicted a major disaster on the Roman people was the first to pay the full penalty. (7) In this way Caesar avenged a private as well as a public wrong, for the Tigurini had killed the general Piso, grandfather of Caesar's father-in-law Piso, in the same battle as Cassius.

After Caesar's victory over the Tigurini, he crossed the Saône and went in pursuit of the rest of the Helvetian forces. The Helvetii thereupon sent Divico, victor over Lucius Cassius in 107, to negotiate for peace.

113.

CAESAR *B.G.* 1.14 (6) Caesar replied that in spite of the outrages committed by the Helvetii he would make peace with them on these conditions: (i) that they give him hostages as a guarantee that they will keep to their promises, (ii) that they make reparation to the Aedui for all the damage done to them and their allies, (iii) that they do the same for the Allobroges. (7) Divico replied that it was the custom, traditional for generations, for the Helvetii to receive, not to give, hostages: the Romans could testify to that.

The negotiations broke down, and so Caesar followed the Helvetii up the river.

114.

CAESAR *B.G.* 1.15 (4) Caesar kept his troops from engaging the enemy, thinking it sufficient for the time being to prevent the Helvetii from collecting food or destroying it for others. (5) So for about a fortnight they advanced with no more than five or six miles between the rearguard of the enemy and the front of the Roman column. 16 (1) Meanwhile Caesar made daily demands

from the Aedui for the corn which they had promised as a state
to supply . . . (4) The Aedui kept on temporizing; the corn was
being collected, was being brought, was actually here, they said.
(5) When Caesar realized that they were putting him off, and the
day on which he would have to distribute corn to the soldiers was
almost upon him, he called together all the leading Aeduans . . .

Caesar was then told by Liscus of the existence of a revolutionary faction
among the Aedui:

115.

CAESAR *B.G.* 1.17 (2) 'With insidious and treacherous arguments
they have been persuading people not to collect the corn they owe.
(3) They say that even if they cannot yet win the leadership of
Gaul, Gallic domination is preferable to Roman; (4) and that the
Romans definitely intend to deprive the Aedui of their liberty
together with all the rest of Gaul, once they have defeated the
Helvetii.'

116.

CAESAR *B.G.* 1.18 (1) Caesar felt that Liscus' words referred by
implication to Dumnorix, the brother of Diviciacus; but as he did
not want too many others present when the matter was discussed,
he quickly dismissed the meeting. Liscus alone he detained (2) and
questioned him further about what he had said in the assembly.
Liscus then spoke with greater confidence and directness; and
when Caesar put the same questions secretly to some others, he
discovered that the story was true: (3) the man concerned was
Dumnorix, a revolutionary of great audacity, very popular with the
masses because of his liberality. For a number of years he had been
able to purchase cheaply the right to collect the harbour dues and
all the other taxes of the Aedui, simply because when he named a
price nobody else dared put in a counter-bid. (4) This had enabled
him to amass a private fortune and also equipped him for large
scale bribery: (5) he maintained at his own expense a large troop of
cavalry which he kept by him (6) and extended his influence over
neighbouring tribes as well as his own country. To strengthen his
position, he had arranged a marriage for his mother with the most

noble and powerful of the Bituriges; (7) he himself had a Helvetian wife and he had married off his half-sister and other female relations to people from different states. (8) This marriage tie made him sympathetic to the Helvetii, and he had personal reasons for hating Caesar and the Romans, whose arrival had diminished his own influence and restored his brother Diviciacus to his former prestige and standing. (9) He had high hopes of obtaining the throne with Helvetian help if anything happened to the Romans, whereas under Roman rule he despaired even of keeping his present position, let alone becoming king. (10) Caesar also learnt in the course of his inquiries that in the cavalry battle which had gone against him a few days before, it had been Dumnorix and his cavalry (sent by the Aedui to help Caesar) who had fled first and so terrified the rest of the cavalry . . . 19 (1) The suspicions implanted by these discoveries were confirmed by certain indisputable facts: Dumnorix had managed the Helvetian migration through Sequani territory; he had arranged for the exchange of hostages, and all this not just without instructions from Caesar or the Aedui but even without their knowledge; and finally the fact that he was being accused by a magistrate of the Aedui gave Caesar, he thought, sufficient grounds for punishing him or ordering the state to do so.

In spite of all these grounds for suspicion, Caesar decided to take no action against Dumnorix. The ostensible reason given in *B.G.* 1.19–20 is that he did not wish to offend Dumnorix' brother Diviciacus, but a later reference (no. **117**) suggests that Caesar may have been playing a double game. When four years later, in 54, Caesar was preparing for his second invasion of Britain, he collected a number of leading Gauls to take with him as hostages.

117.

CAESAR *B.G.* 5.6 (1) Among others was the Aeduan Dumnorix, who has been mentioned before. Caesar was particularly anxious to take him, as he knew all about his revolutionary fervour, his imperial ambitions, his determination and his considerable standing among the Gauls. (2) An additional reason was that Dumnorix in the Aeduan assembly had claimed to have been offered the kingship of the state by Caesar; the Aedui had been very angry at this, but did not dare to send a deputation to Caesar to repudiate or deprecate the claim. Caesar had found out about this from the provincials with whom he was staying.

The decisive battle took place the day after this conference.

118.
CAESAR *B.G.* 1.23 (1) As he was due to distribute rations to his army in two days time and was no more than eighteen miles from Bibracte, much the largest and most wealthy town of the Aedui, he decided next day to look to his commissariat. Turning aside from the path of the Helvetii, he made straight for Bibracte. (2) News of this was brought to the enemy by runaway slaves of Lucius Aemilius who commanded the Gallic cavalry. (3) The Helvetii perhaps thought that the Romans were turning away in fear, the more so as they had not engaged in battle the day before even though they held superior ground; or they were confident of being able to cut the Romans off from their supplies; at any rate they changed their strategy, turned about and began to make provocative attacks on the rear of the Roman column.

> From this a full-scale battle developed, in which large numbers of the Helvetii were killed; others fled to the Lingones who surrendered them on threat of reprisals.

119.
CAESAR *B.G.* 1.28 (3) [After Caesar's victory] he ordered the Helvetii, Tulingi, and Latovici to return to their country from which they had set out; as they had lost all their food and had nothing at home to withstand famine, the Allobroges were told to supply them with corn. Caesar also made the Helvetii restore the towns and villages which they had burnt. (4) He had a particular reason for doing this; he did not want the area which the Helvetii had left to remain unoccupied, in case the Germans who lived on the other side of the Rhine should be tempted by the richness of the land to cross over from their own territory into that of the Helvetii and become neighbours of the Allobroges and the province of Gaul.

120.
CAESAR *B.G.* 1.30 (1) The Helvetian war was over and chieftains

representing almost every state in Gaul came to congratulate Caesar; (2) they realized, so they said, that Caesar in his campaign against the Helvetii had been exacting punishment for the wrongs they had done to the Roman people; and yet things had turned out just as much to the advantage of Gaul as of Rome; (3) for, they said, the Helvetii had left their homes at a time of great prosperity with the intention of making war on the whole of Gaul and acquiring an empire; out of all the vast area available to them, they intended to choose as a place to live in the one which they had adjudged to be the best situated and the most fertile; the other states they hoped to make tributary.

The lack of independent evidence makes it impossible to be certain whether the Helvetii were peaceable in their intentions or not. Caesar says that they claimed to be so (no. 106); on the other hand, the Gallic chieftains accused them of planning to build an empire at the expense of their neighbours (no. 120). Whom are we to believe? Did Caesar in fact have a valid reason for attacking the Helvetii, or does he appear to be anxious to pick a fight at all costs? We may legitimately doubt whether the terms he offered them were made in good faith if, as Divico says (no. 113), he did know about the Helvetian attitude to hostages. In no. 107 he justifies his intervention as avenging an old defeat — but why in that case should he not be content with his victory over the offending Tigurini? He also suggests that if the Helvetii moved westwards they would threaten the security of the Roman allies and encourage Germans to move into the country they had vacated (no. 120). It is true that the Helvetii did cause some damage by their depredations (no. 111), but perhaps even this would have been avoided if they had been given a free passage.

THE GERMANS

The defeat of the Helvetii left Caesar with another month of campaigning time; if possible, it would obviously be to his political advantage to score another major victory before the year was at an end. The most obvious opponents were the Gallic enemies of the Aedui and their German overlords. According to Caesar's account, it was at this stage that the Gallic chieftains invited him to attend a conference at which they told him about the first German incursions across the Rhine and asked for his help in getting rid of them (see no. 97). It is almost unthinkable that Caesar should not have known about the situation until now; after all, he had been instrumental in making Ariovistus a 'Friend of the Roman People' the year before (B.G. 1.35.2). But he needed a pretext for turning on him now and goes to considerable length in his account to make it seem plausible. Ariovistus, not surprisingly, regarded his Gallic territory as fairly won and Caesar's interference as unwarranted.

121.

CAESAR *B.G.* 1.33 (1) [When Caesar had listened to the pleas for assistance against the Germans — see no. **97**,] he promised to look into the matter, and gave the Gauls some encouragement by saying that he had high hopes of putting an end to Ariovistus' mischief, because of the favours he had shown him and the authority he held over him. (2) With these words he dismissed the assembly. Now there were many factors leading Caesar to suppose that he ought to take deliberate action; [etc. as in no. **96**] . . . (5) As for Ariovistus, he took on such airs and was so arrogant as to be almost insufferable.

> The Cimbri and Teutones were traditional 'bogeymen' whose names were used to frighten the public, but there is reason to believe that the Romans brought some of the trouble on themselves (see no. **122**).

122.

APPIAN *Celt.* 13. A large band of Teutones attacked the land of Noreia, intent on plunder. The Roman consul Papirius Carbo [in 113] was afraid that they might attack Italy, and so laid an ambush in the Alps where the pass is narrowest. When they made no move in that direction, he went out after them himself on the pretext that the Noreians who had been attacked were under the patronage of Rome. . . . As Carbo approached, the Teutones sent word that they had not known about this Roman patronage of Noricum and would stay away in future. Carbo received the envoys politely and offered the Teutones guides for the journey home. However he gave the guides secret instructions to take them round by a longer route. Meanwhile he cut across country and without warning fell upon the Teutones as they were still resting. However he paid for his treachery by losing many of his troops. . . . And the Teutones continued their journey into Gaul.

> Caesar first suggested that he and Ariovistus should meet for discussions.

123.

CAESAR *B.G.* 1.34 (2) Ariovistus replied: 'If I want anything from you, I will come and see you; but if you want anything from me, you'll have to come yourself . . . (4) Anyway I don't really see what business you or the Roman people have in the part of Gaul which is mine by right of conquest.'

Caesar replied with an ultimatum:

124.

CAESAR *B.G.* 1.35 (3) . . . (i) he was not to bring any more of his hordes across the Rhine into Gaul; (ii) he was to give up his Aeduan hostages; (iii) he was to give the Sequani permission to return their hostages as well; (iv) he was not to aggravate the Aedui, or make war on them or their allies. (4) 'If you do this, you may continue to enjoy the favour and friendship of the Roman people for ever. But if not, then I shall not let the wrongs done to the Aedui go unpunished; for in the year when Marcus Messalla and Marcus Piso were consuls [etc. as in no. **94**]. . . .'

125.

CAESAR *B.G.* 1.37 (1) On the same day that Caesar heard of Ariovistus' rejection of his ultimatum, representatives of the Aedui and the Treveri arrived. (2) The Aedui complained that their land was being devastated by the Harudes who had recently crossed into Gaul; not even the hostages they had sent to Ariovistus could secure peace. (3) The Treveri brought news that one hundred Suebian clans had arrived at the banks of the Rhine led by the brothers Nasua and Cimberius, to try and cross the river. (4) Caesar was seriously worried by this information and decided upon prompt action; resistance would be difficult if these new bands of Suebians joined forces with Ariovistus' veterans. (5) So he arranged his food supplies as quickly as he could and marched at speed against Ariovistus.

Hearing that Ariovistus was heading for Vesontio (Besançon), Caesar forestalled him by occupying the town. Here his soldiers became apprehensive at the thought of facing these fearsome Germans (*B.G.* 1.39.1); there may also have been other reasons for their unease, not recorded by Caesar.

126.

DIO 38.35 (1) News came that Ariovistus was making strenuous preparations and that many other Germans had either crossed the river already to help him, or had collected on the bank to make a sudden attack on the Romans. This caused great despondency. (2) They were terrified by the obvious menace of the enemy's size and numbers, and almost inclined to think that they were going out to fight savage and unpredictable animals rather than men. The soldiers muttered that the war was no business of theirs; it had not been officially sanctioned and was only being fought because of Caesar's personal ambition. If he did not change his mind, they threatened to desert.

This was Caesar's reply to the malcontents:

127.
CAESAR *B.G.* 1.40 (3) 'I am convinced that, when he has understood my demands and realized how fair are my terms, he will not forfeit my good-will or that of the Roman people. (4) But if some lunatic frenzy drives him to make war on us, what have we to fear?'

Caesar's diplomatic handling averted a mutiny and enabled him to catch up Ariovistus' army after a week's hard marching.

Ariovistus proposed another parley, and Caesar repeated the terms of his ultimatum. To this Ariovistus replied (*B.G.* 1.44): that he had been invited into Gaul, and the hostages had been given voluntarily; that the Gauls had made war on him, not he on them; that the Germans he had brought with him were for defensive, not offensive, purposes; that the Germans had more right to that part of Gaul than the Romans did; that the Aedui, in spite of being 'brothers' of the Romans, had neither received help from them nor given any . . .

128.
CAESAR *B.G.* 1.44 (10) 'I am bound to suspect, Caesar, that your friendship is a sham and that your army here in Gaul is for no other purpose than to crush me. (11) So if you do not get out of this area and take your army with you, I shall treat you not as a friend but as an enemy; (12) and if I kill you, I shall give great satisfaction to a large number of noble and distinguished Roman citizens. This I know for a fact from all the messages sent to me by people offering favour and friendship at the price of your death. (13) But if you leave the country and let me have free possession of Gaul, I shall

be liberal in my gratitude and will carry out any campaigns you might wish with no trouble or danger to yourself.'

Caesar replied that he would not give up the allies and that the Romans had in fact got priority rights in Gaul. Negotiations were broken off, and, when Ariovistus tried to reopen them, Caesar refused to attend in person. The Gaul he sent to represent him was flung into prison by Ariovistus. Thereupon battle was joined; the Germans were thoroughly defeated and fled back across the Rhine.

129.

CAESAR *B.G.* 1.54 (1) When news of this battle had reached the far side of the Rhine, the Suebi who were on the bank began to turn back home; as they fled in terror, the Ubii who live next to the Rhine attacked and killed a large number of them. (2) Caesar, after completing two major campaigns in a single season, now put his army into winter quarters among the Sequani earlier than the time of year required, leaving Labienus in charge. (3) He himself went off to make his tour of Cisalpine Gaul.

Later writers were by no means agreed about the validity of Caesar's reasons for undertaking the German campaign.

130.

FLORUS 1.45 (9) The Rhine was not left free of attack; for it was quite wrong that the enemy should use it as a safe refuge and defence. (10) The first battle fought on it against the Germans was totally justified. Their incursions gave rise to complaints from the Aedui. (11) And then, the arrogance of Ariovistus! When envoys told him to come to Caesar, he said 'Who is Caesar? If he wants anything, he will have to come here. What concern is it of his what we in Germany do? (12) You don't see me interfering in Roman affairs do you?' So great was the alarm inspired by these strange new people that everywhere soldiers were making their wills, even in the middle of the camp.

131.

DIO 38.34 (3) Ariovistus was the king of these Germans; he had had his position as king confirmed by the Romans and had been enrolled as a friend and ally by the consul, Caesar himself. But

Caesar thought nothing of this in comparison with the glory and power which would result from the campaign, and turned his attention to finding a pretext for quarrelling and putting the blame on Ariovistus so that he should not appear as the aggressor himself.

The account of the negotiations leading up to the attack on Ariovistus bears some resemblance to that preceding the Helvetian campaign: in each case Caesar quotes a defeat to be avenged (regardless of who had been the aggressor), issues an ultimatum which is quite unacceptable and learns of overtly hostile action by the enemy (the Helvetian depredations in no. **111** and the incursions of the Harudes in no. **125**) after he has already decided to attack. Are these signs of a weakness in Caesar's case? Florus maintained that the campaign was totally justified (no. **130**); Dio on the other hand felt that Ariovistus was the victim of Caesar's ambition. Which is the more likely to be right?

THE BELGAE

The placing of Caesar's legions in winter quarters among the Sequani could be interpreted as a sensible precaution after the events of 58, or as deliberately provocative to the other Gallic tribes. At any rate the effect was to drive the Belgians into a defensive alliance, which Caesar spent the whole of his next campaigning season (summer 57) in breaking up. His continuous victories against these reputedly formidable opponents finally won for him the acknowledgement from Rome that he wanted.

132.

(The first reference to the Belgians in the introduction to Bk. 1.)

CAESAR *B.G.* 1.1 (4) The Belgians are the most courageous of all the Gallic tribes, because they are the furthest away from the civilizing influence of the Province. Even traders only go there very infrequently, and this limits the importation of goods which might have a softening effect on them. They are also nearest to the Germans living across the Rhine, with whom they are constantly at war.

If this was originally part of Caesar's first despatch from Gaul, it would have reached Rome in winter 58/57, a timely advertisement for his forthcoming campaign.

133.

CAESAR *B.G.* 2.1 (1) When Casar was in Cisalpine Gaul as we have said [cf. no. **129**], he heard numerous reports, later confirmed by

Labienus' letters, that all the Belgians, whom we have already described as being a third of Gaul, were forming a conspiracy against the Roman people and exchanging hostages. (2) These were the reasons for the conspiracy: one, they were afraid that the Roman army might be directed against them, now that the whole of Gaul was pacified; (3) two, there were a number of Gallic agitators at work; some who had objected to the continued presence of the Germans in Gaul and were no less indignant at the Roman army staying on and wintering there; others whose unstable ideas always made them enthusiastic revolutionaries; (4) and others still who felt that they were less likely to realize their dynastic ambitions under Roman rule (for in Gaul the rule was usually held by the most powerful and persuasive people).

Caesar recruited two new legions and joined the rest of his army. The Remi at once offered help and provided further information about the different Belgian tribes (B.G. 2.4). He defeated the main Belgian army at Bibrax (B.G. 2.5–11), then secured the submission of the Suessiones (B.G. 2.12) and the Bellovaci (B.G. 2.13–15). His most dangerous encounter was with the Nervii who nearly won a surprise victory in an attack on the Roman camp (B.G. 2.15–28). When they and the Aduatuci, who had been coming to help them, had finally surrendered (B.G. 2.29–33), Caesar could regard his conquest of the Belgians as complete. His lieutenants meanwhile had been equally successful.

134.
CAESAR B.G. 2.34 Meanwhile Crassus had been sent with a single legion to the maritime states on the Atlantic coast, the Veneti, Venelli, Osismi, Curiosolites, Esubii, Aulerci, and Redones. Now he reported that these states had been brought to recognize the sovereignty and power of the Roman people.

135.
CAESAR B.G. 2.35 (1) These achievements completed the pacification of Gaul . . . (3) Caesar then left for Italy, after placing his legions in winter-quarters among the Carnutes, Andes, Turones and other states adjacent to the scene of his latest operations. (4) When his despatches reached Rome he was awarded the unprecedented honour of a fortnight's public thanksgiving in recognition of his achievements.

All the winter quarters were in north-west Gaul; this and the expedition of Crassus (no. **134**) are the first indications of a possible interest in crossing the Channel.

How did Caesar come to be awarded a thanksgiving at the end of this year rather than the one preceding?

B. Illyria

Caesar's Illyrian province is easily forgotten in face of his achievements in Gaul, but it had been assigned to him before Transalpine Gaul and it did offer immediate prospects of conquest (see nos. **82** ff.); what is more, at the beginning of his command he had three legions stationed at Aquileia, the natural starting point for any campaign beyond the north-east frontier.

136.

CAESAR *B.G.* 1.10 (3) Caesar hurried to Italy with all speed. There he enrolled two legions and collected from their winter-quarters the legions which had been wintering at Aquileia. With these five he took the shortest route to Transalpine Gaul through the Alps [sc. to begin his Helvetian campaign].

After the Belgian campaign Caesar regarded the conquest of Gaul as virtually complete (see below), and he could take another look at the Illyrian situation. As a preliminary he sent Galba to open a route through the Alps which would give his troops direct access to Cisalpine Gaul and beyond, while he himself conducted a personal reconnaissance (winter 57/6).

137.

CAESAR *B.G.* 3.1 (1) As Caesar was on his way to Italy, he sent Servius [Sulpicius] Galba with the twelfth legion and part of the cavalry into the land of the Nantuates, Veragri, and Seduni who occupy territory bordered by the Allobroges and enclosed by Lake Geneva, the Rhône, and the highest Alps. (2) The reason for sending him was a desire to open up the old route through the Alps which traders had once used at great personal risk and on payment of heavy dues. (3) He gave Servius permission to place his legion in winter-quarters there if he thought the situation demanded it. (4) Servius fought several successful battles and captured a number of the enemy's forts; when they had all sent envoys to negotiate, he exacted hostages and concluded peace. He then decided to place two cohorts among the Nantuates, while he himself wintered with the rest of the legion in a village of the Veragri called Octodurus ... 2 (5) [However the Gauls then decided to reopen the campaign,] because they were convinced that the Romans were not only interested in the road; they were trying to get permanent possession of the Alpine peaks and add this region to their nearby province ... 6 (4) Even though he succeeded in beating off the new attack, Galba was reluctant to tempt fortune too often; things had turned out very differently from the way he had intended when he came into winter-quarters, and he was seriously worried by a shortage of food and supplies. So on the next day, after burning all the buildings in the village, he hurried back to the Province.

138.

CAESAR *B.G.* 3.7 (1) With the campaign completed, Caesar thought for many reasons that Gaul was pacified — the Belgians had been crushed, the Germans driven out, and the Seduni defeated in the Alps; so at the beginning of winter he set out for Illyricum, as he wanted to make first-hand acquaintance with those people as well and get to know the area.

Caesar's presence in Aquileia is confirmed by a reference in Cic. *Vat.* 38 (see no. **174**) and by a recently published inscription which gives a precise date:

139.
SALONA DECREE

> v. (1)   In the consulship of Gnaius Lentulus Mar-
> -cellinus and Lucius Marcius Philip-
> -pus on the third of Mar-
>
> (4) -ch ...
>
> (9) In Aquileia in the presence of Gaius Julius Caesar
> the commander in chief, Gaius Gavenius son of Gaius (?)
> Fabia held talks about the

    (12) freedom of the people of Issa and the friendship (?)
        between Rome and Issa

Issa is an island (now Vis) some 30 miles south-west of Split.

In the end these preparations led nowhere: perhaps Caesar's own findings
had been unpropitious, perhaps Galba's failure made access too difficult,
or perhaps he was genuinely forestalled by the result of the Veneti. At
any rate, he only visited the province once more during his governorship,
in the winter of 54/3, and that simply to deal with depredations such as
might be expected to result from his neglect of the area (*B.G.* 5.1.5–9). A
more serious outbreak occurred in 52 when the town of Tergeste (Trieste)
was overrun by Illyrians, and Caesar, preoccupied with Vercingetorix'
revolt, could do nothing about it (see no. **348** with App. *Ill.* 18). In the
end therefore Caesar made little use of this province, although a continued
interest in it is indicated by the campaigning plans interrupted by his
death (see nos. **86–90, 391, 397**).

An independent view of Caesar's Illyrian command:

140.
APPIAN *Ill.* 15. I find it remarkable that so many great Roman
armies should have made their way through the Alps to fight
Gauls and Spaniards, and paid no attention to these people [sc.
the Illyrians]; even Caesar, who was a most successful campaigner,
did nothing about them in his ten years of fighting the Gauls in
spite of the fact that he wintered near the country. Actually the
other commanders seem only to have had thoughts for crossing
the Alps in pursuit of their appointed objective; while Caesar was
more concerned with affairs in Gaul, and that, with the Pompeian
civil war which followed it, delayed his settlement of the Illyrian
situation. For he was apparently appointed to command Illyria as
well as the Gauls — not the whole of Illyria, but all that belonged
to the Romans at the time.

Appian alone of our ancient sources raises the question why Caesar lost
interest in an Illyrian campaign. Perhaps we could go some way to
supplying an explanation by asking when he first contemplated the
complete conquest of Gaul.

IV. The Renewal of the Partnership

Caesar's military successes against Ariovistus and the Belgians had brought him unprecedented honours and, what was even more important, implicit acknowledgement by the Senate of the legality of his position. In granting him a public thanksgiving they silenced for a while the extreme conservatives who had hoped to depose Caesar from his command on the ground that it had been unconstitutionally acquired. This still did not mean that Caesar's political position in Rome was assured; in fact it was considerably more precarious at the end of 57 than it had been two years earlier when he ended his consulship. The new danger came not so much from the Senate as from his own partners in power.

The political alliance which Caesar had formed with Pompey and Crassus in December 59 (see nos. 12 ff.) had been based on expediency alone. There was too much self-interest involved to hope that the partnership would long remain stable. Once Pompey and Crassus had, through Caesar's influence, satisfied their immediate needs, what prospects of advancement remained to them? They could see that their prestige and money were being used to further Caesar's own career, with no corresponding advantage to themselves. The only foreseeable end to such a relationship was complete subordination. Whether or not this was Caesar's intention, a breach in the partnership was precipitated by the open hostility of Clodius which drove Pompey to seek the friendship and patronage of the *optimates*. For his efforts on their behalf the Senate rewarded Pompey with the first command he had held since his return from Asia, although they baulked at the idea of putting an army into his hands. For the time being he had to be content that his self-respect had been restored.

If Caesar was worried by Pompey's disaffection, he had also to think of his own position: the subjugation of the Belgians had completed the pacification of Gaul, and yet he still had half of his five-year allocation to run. What should he do? Return to Rome straightaway, or look for new areas to conquer? Whatever he did, he could not yet afford to drop his partners and in April 56 he called them into conference at Luca to make some arrangements for the future. The proceedings were so secretive that some of our principal sources make no mention of the meeting at all; in fact it is only from circumstantial evidence that we can hope to reconstruct the intentions of Caesar in calling the meeting and the outcome of the negotiations which were held there. Of its importance there is no doubt, since it brought about at any rate a temporary reconciliation between the partners; this in turn protected Caesar from fear of attack at Rome and enabled him to extend his command for an extra five years, during which the whole of Gaul came into his hands.

A. The alienation of Pompey

THE TIGRANES AFFAIR

Clodius' high-handed behaviour made him many enemies, and not all of them were enemies of Caesar as well. His abduction of the young Tigranes, one of Pompey's most important hostages, was a characteristic act of spite, bringing no great advantage to himself and causing considerable offence to Pompey. The only concrete result was to strengthen the cause of the *optimates* working for Cicero's recall, and it leaves us wondering what Clodius' motives were and for whom he thought he was working. For detailed discussion of this problem, see the Bibliography under *Clodius*.

141.

ASCONIUS *in Milon* p. 47. After his triumph over Mithridates, Pompey had put the son of Tigranes into chained custody at the house of the senator Flavius. Flavius became praetor the same year as Clodius was tribune [58], and Clodius asked him over dinner one day if he would have Tigranes sent in so that he could have a look at him. When he was brought, Clodius gave him a place at the table and then refused to hand him back; he sent him to his own house where he kept him free of chains and refused all Pompey's demands for his return.

Even Cicero was a little surprised at the fickleness of Clodius' allegiance:

142.

CICERO *Dom.* 66. As evidence that Clodius' hatred was always directed not against certain individuals, but against good qualities in general, just remember that after my banishment and Cato's removal he rounded on the very man whose initiative and assistance had both in the past and at the present moment, as he himself admitted, enabled him to act as he did at public meetings.

143.

DIO 38.30 (1) Cicero's exile did not last long, as he was restored by Pompey, the very man who had been chiefly responsible for his banishment. This was the reason: Clodius had been bribed to release Tigranes the younger, after stealing him from the house of Lucius Flavius where he was imprisoned. (2) When Pompey and Gabinius objected, he treated them with contempt, severely beating up a number of their supporters and breaking the consul's *fasces* and confiscating his property. (3) Pompey was furious, especially as Clodius was using against him the authority which he personally restored to the tribunes [as consul in 70]. He therefore determined to recall Cicero and immediately set in motion the wheels for his restoration through Ninnius (cf. nos. **146** ff.)

Who might have been responsible for bribing Clodius?

144.

PLUTARCH *Pomp.* 48 (6) When Clodius saw that his popular measures had succeeded in winning him the support of the people, he at once set about undoing some of Pompey's arrangements: he stole away his prisoner, Tigranes, and kept him at his own house; and he brought charges against Pompey's friends, to make a test of his power . . . 49 (1) Pompey naturally resented this defamation and this kind of campaigning, which was quite new to him. But he was even more hurt to see the Senate gloating at his distress and the retribution for his betrayal of Cicero. (2) When there were outbreaks of violence in the forum, resulting in serious injury, and when one of Clodius' men was caught sword in hand, stealing through a crowd of bystanders in the direction of Pompey, then he made this an excuse not to come into the forum in the rest of Clodius' year of office. In fact he was just as much afraid of Clodius' wanton abuse. Instead he stayed at home, discussing with his friends possible ways of mollifying the anger felt against him by the Senate and *optimates*. (3) [Q. Terentius] Culleo [one of the tribunes] suggested that he should divorce Julia and make friends with the Senate instead of Caesar, but Pompey refused and preferred the idea of bringing back Cicero, who was Clodius' greatest enemy and the Senate's greatest friend.

For similar timidity on the part of Pompey, see no. **303.**

Cicero himself hoped that the affair would be enough to disrupt the partnership:

145.

CICERO *ad Att.* 3.8 [Thessalonica, 29 May 58] (3) Now to the points in your letter . . . I see you have been talking with Pompey. But I don't see any possibility of the great political upheaval which you envisage — or are you just suggesting it to console me? If Pompey doesn't do anything about Tigranes, the chance is lost . . . (4) I am sending you a copy of the letter I have been writing to Pompey.

THE RECALL OF CICERO

For Pompey the easiest way back into favour with the *optimates* was by helping to promote the recall of Cicero from exile, even if, as he must have known, all efforts during that year were bound to founder on the veto of Clodius or other tribunes.

146.

CICERO *ad Att.* 3.10 [Thessalonica, 17 June 58] (1) If there are any hopeful signs of action, I shall either stay here or come over and join you. But if 'hopes are fading', I shall look elsewhere. So far the only news I have been given is about the dissension in the ranks of the powers that be; but their disagreement seems to be over everything but me, so I don't know what good I shall get out of it.

147.

CICERO *Sest.* 67. Finally, later than he might have wished . . . Gnaius Pompeius resurrected his tradition of service to the state. 68. . . . He joined himself to the cause of the state; he used his authority to bring proceedings to a halt and protest at what had already taken place. A new note of optimism was apparent. On the first of June a crowded Senate unanimously passed a decree about my return, at the proposal of Lucius Ninnius, whose loyalty and courage on my behalf have never wavered (see nos. **52, 143**). Then a veto interposed by that . . . that nonentity [Aelius] Ligus, that excrescence from the ranks of my enemies.

Ninnius and Ligus were both tribunes.

148.

CICERO *ad Att*. 3.12 [Thessalonica, 17 July 58] (1) You have certainly been at pains to argue what we may hope for, especially from the Senate; but then you tell me that Clodius has published the clause in the bill forbidding any reference to the subject in the Senate. So of course nobody does ... You say that things will be more promising after the elections [at the end of the month]. But what difference will it make, with the same tribune in office and my enemy consul designate [sc. Q. Caecilius Metellus Nepos]?

As Cicero suspected, the elections made no difference (*ad Att*. 3.13.1) and even his supporters were unwilling to take action without consulting Caesar, whose attitude was still unhelpful.

149.

CICERO *Sest*. 71. At this stage, when Publius Sestius had just been elected tribune, he set off to see Gaius Caesar about my welfare. What he did and how far he succeeded have nothing to do with the case (though, in my opinion, if Caesar was favourably disposed towards me, as I think, Sestius was unsuccessful; if less favourably disposed, he was only moderately successful).

150.

CICERO *ad Att*. 3.18 [Thessalonica, c. 10 Sept. 58] (1) You raised my hopes considerably with your news that Varro had assured you as a friend that Pompey was definitely going to take up my case and would find someone to act for him as soon as he had received from Caesar the reply he was expecting. Was there nothing in this? Was Caesar's letter unfavourable, or is there still a hope?

In spite of Clodius' obstruction senatorial pressure was mounting. Both Sestius and the leading anti-Caesarian, Lucius Domitius, had publicized their intention of taking legislative action (*ad Att*. 3.20.3, 3.15.6). Then in October eight tribunes made a formal proposal for Cicero's recall (*ad Att*. 3.23.1); but, as Cicero himself realized, it was little more than a gesture, with no greater immunity from veto than the earlier recommendation of the Senate. In the new year another attempt was made (*ad Att*. 3.26, Jan. 57); but this was thwarted by the delaying tactics of the tribune Atilius Serranus (Cic. *Sest*. 74), and Cicero again lapsed into deep gloom (*ad Att*. 3.27). In the end he had to wait a further six months before the decree could be passed. Opinions differed about what part Caesar had played in the final decision.

151.

DIO 39.6 (1) Meanwhile Pompey engineered the vote for Cicero's recall . . . (2) He was supported by a number of praetors and tribunes, including Titus Annius Milo; these were instrumental in bringing the measure before the people. In the Senate he was also helped by the consul [P. Cornelius Lentulus] Spinther who was motivated partly by a desire to win Pompey's favour, partly by a private grudge against Clodius which had earlier led him to vote for Clodius' condemnation at his trial for adultery. (3) On the other side were a number of magistrates including Clodius' brother (the praetor Appius Claudius) and the consul Metellus Nepos, who had private grounds for hating Cicero.

152.

DIO 39.10 (1) Caesar and Crassus really did not like Cicero, but they showed some interest in him when they realized that that he was bound to be restored whatever happened. Caesar, in spite of being away in Gaul, showed that he was quite well-disposed towards him, but neither he nor Crassus received any thanks in return.

> To what extent was Caesar responsible for securing Cicero's recall? See nos. **149** f., **153.**

153.

CICERO *Pis.* 80. When Gnaius Pompeius devoted all his energy and interest to me, even at the risk of his own life, by approaching the provincial towns on my behalf, begging Italy for loyal support, associating constantly with the consul Lentulus, the champion of my cause, publicizing the opinion of the Senate and acknowledging the role of upholder of my restoration as well as that of intercessor on my behalf; then, to support and assist his cause, he took onto his side a man whose influence he knew to be great and whose relations with me he had discovered to be not unfriendly — Gaius Caesar.

> Was Cicero deceiving himself about Pompey's enthusiasm? Compare this account with those given by Dio and Plutarch (nos. **143** f., **151**).

154.

CICERO *ad Att.* 4.1 [Rome, c. 10 Sept. 57] (4) I left Dyrrachium on August 4th, the very day on which the proposal about me was put to the vote. I arrived at Brundisium on the 5th. . . . While there, I had a letter from my brother Quintus describing how the law had been carried in the Centuriate Assembly, with a wonderful display of enthusiasm from people of every age and rank, and an incredible gathering from all parts of the country.

POMPEY'S COMMAND OF THE CORN-SUPPLY

Immediately after Cicero had returned to Rome, Pompey was rewarded with a senatorial decree giving him the power to administer the corn-supply throughout the empire. Both the circumstances and the timing of this measure gave rise to suspicions, even among his contemporaries, that the reasons for it were more political than economic.

155.

CICERO *ad Att.* 4.1 [Rome, c. 10 Sept. 57] (5) On the next day, September 5th, I attended the Senate and expressed my thanks. (6) On these two days the price of bread rose sharply, and people were running first to the Theatre, then to the Senate, crying out that the corn-shortage was my fault. Clodius had put them up to this. The Senate met to discuss the matter, while public opinion, among the *optimates* as well as the people, demanded that Pompey should be put in charge of the situation. He was in favour of this himself, and, as there was popular pressure on me to propose it, I obliged in a carefully prepared speech. In the absence of all the ex-consuls except [M. Valerius] Messalla and Afranius, who alone were not afraid to vote, a senatorial decree was passed according to my proposal that Pompey should be approached about undertaking this charge, and a law made. When the bill was read out, the people applauded loudly at the mention of my name — a tasteless new habit of theirs. . . . (7) On the next day there was a full house in the Senate, including all the ex-consuls, prepared to grant anything Pompey wanted. He asked for a committee of fifteen with me at their head, saying that I would be his other self in all matters. The consul drafted a law giving Pompey complete control of the corn-supplies throughout the whole world for a period of five years; Messius added an amendment giving him complete financial control, a fleet and an army, and authority to go over the heads of the provincial governors even in their own provinces. The consular law seems to be quite reasonable and Pompey says he prefers it; but his friends say he would rather have the quite intolerable proposal of Messius. The consular party with Favonius at their head loudly oppose it. I'm keeping quiet.

> According to Dio 39.9.2 the citizens threatened to burn the Senate and the whole of the Capitol. For a more rhetorical account of the part played by Cicero, see Cic. *Dom.* 16–19.

Cicero suggested these reasons for a corn-shortage in summer 57:

156.

CICERO *Dom.* 11. Partly because the corn-growing provinces were short of grain; partly because they had exported it elsewhere — thanks to the extortionate demands of the dealers, do you think? — ; partly because the store-keepers locked it away, hoping to win more thanks when they came to the rescue in times of real famine and released it unexpectedly.

Political motives suggested for Pompey's command:

157.

PLUTARCH *Pomp.* 49 (4) When Cicero was recalled by law, he immediately reconciled Pompey with the Senate and, in the debate on the corn-law, persuaded them to make him as it were master of all the land and sea under Roman dominion. For under his charge were placed all the harbours, markets and food-supplies, in fact everything related to navigation and agriculture. (5) Clodius complained that the law had not been brought in because of the food-shortage, but that the food-shortage had been brought about so that the law would have to be passed. . . . Others suggest that this was an ingenious idea of the consul Spinther, to hamstring Pompey with a higher command so that he himself could be sent to the assistance of Ptolemy [see nos. **164** ff.].

> Cicero's account, being contemporary, ought to have the more authority. Is it also the more plausible? Why should Plutarch have chosen not to accept it?

CLODIUS AND MILO

Even though Clodius' tribunate ended in Dec. 58, he was no less influential a figure the following year when his armed gangs openly challenged constitutional authority. Pompey, hoping to win further credit as the champion of civil law and order, was not afraid to oppose violence with violence — so long as someone else did the dirty work. His chosen instrument was Titus Annius Milo, a tribune in 57, who now began a running battle with Clodius which was to last five years.

158.

APPIAN *B.C.* 2.15 (58) [After exiling Cicero] Clodius was so elated that he was tempted to compare himself with Pompey, who was still the most powerful man in the city. 16 (59) So Pompey encouraged Milo — a colleague of Clodius in office, and an even more reckless adventurer — with hopes of a consulship and persuaded him to have Cicero recalled by law in spite of Clodius' opposition. He hoped that when Cicero returned he would forget what he had suffered from the party in power and, instead of speaking about them, would bring trouble and retribution upon Clodius.

159.

DIO 39.7 (3) Clodius was feared by everyone and now made a bid for the aedileship, hoping that if elected he would be able to escape retribution for his use of violence. (4) Milo did in fact bring a charge against him, but never got him into court. The main reason for the hold-up was this: the quaestors, who are responsible for selecting jurors, had not yet been chosen, and [Metellus] Nepos forbade the praetor to allow any trial before the jurors had been picked; however the quaestors couldn't be elected before the aediles.

160.

CICERO *ad Att.* 4.3 [Rome, Nov. 57] (3) Clodius threatened the city with reprisals if his election did not take place. Milo brought forward the proposal which he had had in writing at the time of his speech — that the trial should include a hearing of all my complaints against eviction, arson, and assault, and that this should take place before the election; meanwhile Milo made it known that he was going to observe the heavens on every election day, if the the trial were not held first. [The initial success of this manoeuvre prompted Cicero to prophesy:] (5) I don't think the elections will take place; I expect Clodius will be put on trial by Milo — or of course he may be killed first: I can see that Milo would lose no opportunity of doing away with him if a riot offered him the chance.

Cicero was wrong: Clodius did manage to get himself elected and once out of harm's way even made an attack on Caesar.

161

CICERO *Dom.* 40. When your tribunate was already crumbling in ruins, you suddenly came forward as champion of the auspices. You brought Bibulus and the augurs to a public meeting; the augurs, in answer to your question, said that it was illegal to do anything in the assembly when the heavens were being observed; and Bibulus, when asked, . . . said that you had never really been a proper tribune, as you had been adopted in the face of the auspices. Finally, in the later months of your office, you were behind the whole move to get the legislation of Caesar rescinded on the ground that it had been passed in defiance of the auspices; and if that happened, you said you would carry me back shoulder-high to Rome as guardian of the city.

Are we to believe Clodius or Cicero — or neither?

Cicero of course approved of all that Milo did to oppose Clodius, whatever the means.

162.

CICERO *post Red. in Sen.* 19. First he tried to bring a charge against Clodius for assault. Then when he realized that the would-be defendant had made judicial proceedings impossible, he did his best to prevent Clodius determining everything by violence.

163.

DIO 39.8 (1) Finally Milo himself collected a gang of gladiators and sympathizers; there was then a continual series of clashes with

Clodius' men, and bloodshed was widespread through just about the whole city.

THE EGYPTIAN QUESTION

Although Pompey's prestige was restored by his new command, he still had no army to balance the weight of Caesar's legions. For a month or two it looked as if he might even get this when the Egyptian king, Ptolemy Auletes (i.e. Flute-player), came to Rome with the promise of enormous rewards to anyone who would restore him to the throne from which his subjects had deposed him (Dio 39.12.1–3). The offer was too tempting to be allowed to fall to Pompey uncontested: among others, Crassus saw hopes for himself in it, and there might have been a dangerous confrontation had not the Senate opportunely discovered an oracle in the Sibylline Books which forbade the use of an army in restoring a king of Egypt (Dio 39.15.1–2).

Another of the main contenders for the assignment was Lentulus Spinther, in 56 proconsul in Cilicia. As consul the preceding year, he had been instrumental in having Cicero recalled, and Cicero felt under some obligation to return the compliment (cf. nos. **151, 153**).

164.

CICERO *ad Fam.* 1.1 [Rome, 13 Jan. 56, to P. Lentulus Spinther] (1) Ammonius, the king's envoy, is using bribes to thwart us, quite openly . . . Those who support the king — and there aren't many of them — all want the matter put in the hands of Pompey. The Senate is prepared to accept the fiction of religious scruples, not for any genuine religious reasons but out of spite and dislike for the king's use of bribery . . . (3) This is what has happened so far (I'm writing this early on the morning of the 13th): Hortensius, Lucullus and I are prepared to accept the religious objections to the use of an army (there's no way round that in any case); but, along the lines of the senatorial decree already passed on your motion, we support the proposal to send you to restore the king 'in so far as you can do so without harm to the state'. This would mean that the Senate leaves the matter in your hands, in spite of the religious scruple removing the army. Crassus supports the idea of three commissioners, selected if need be even from people already holding a command, and therefore not excluding Pompey. Bibulus proposes the election of three commissioners specifically from those *not* holding a command. The other ex-consuls agree with Bibulus' proposal, except Servilius [Isauricus, cons. 79] who says that the king should not be restored at all; Volcatius who, on Lupus' motion, supports the appointment of Pompey, and Afranius who takes the same line. This leads us to suspect that Pompey really would like the assignment, as his friends, significantly, agree with Volcatius.

> Why was the Ptolemy affair made into such a political issue, and what light did it shed on current political affiliations? For Cicero it meant the embarrassment of divided loyalties, neither of which he was prepared to abandon (cf. nos. 242 ff., 267).

165.

CICERO *ad Q.f.* 2.2 [Rome, 17 Jan. 56] (3) In the affair of the Alexandrian king, a senatorial decree has been passed saying that 'it would be dangerous to the state's interests to effect his restoration with a large body of men.' This left the Senate to decide whether Lentulus or Pompey should take charge of the restoration. Lentulus seemed to be winning his case, and in the debate I made a remarkably fine job of fulfilling my obligations to him, while brilliantly accommodating the wishes of Pompey. But Lentulus' opponents put up a number of bogus objections to hinder his case . . . There seems to be no doubt that he is a lost cause, and I am heartily sorry.

166.

CICERO *ad Fam.* 1.4 [Rome, Jan. 56, to P. Lentulus, proconsul] (1) On Jan. 15th we were beautifully placed in the Senate, having smashed Bibulus' proposals about the three commissioners on the day before [the meetings of the Senate on Jan. 13th and 14th are described fully in *ad Fam.* 1.2]; that only left the proposal of Volcatius to argue about, but the debate was held up through the numerous bogus objections raised by our opponents . . . You know that the *Lex Pupia* prevents the Senate meeting before the first of February, and of course the whole of February is ruled out, unless the business with foreign representatives is either finished off or postponed. (2) It is widely supposed here that the fictitious device of the religious scruple was not introduced by your spiteful opponents to hinder you particularly, but to prevent anyone wanting to go to Alexandria for the sake of getting a military command.

> By law the Senate had to devote the whole of February to receiving foreign deputations, and as they were not allowed to meet at all in the second half of January, this meant that the whole question had to be shelved for six weeks. During that time there was only one false alarm when Cato threatened to deprive Lentulus of his province (Cic. *ad Fam.* 1.5a.2, *ad Q.f.* 2.3.1).

Pompey was losing interest and was more immediately concerned with Clodius' attempt to prosecute Milo for assault (see nos. **169** ff.).

167.

CICERO *ad Fam.* 1.5b [Rome, Feb. 56, to Lentulus Spinther] (1) When Pompey made a public speech in defence of Milo on Feb. 6th, he was subjected to abusive barracking, and later in the Senate Cato made rude and offensive allegations against him. His friends remained absolutely silent, and Pompey himself looked to be in considerable distress. So it looks as if he has well and truly given up the Alexandrian affair — though as far as we are concerned the position is unchanged and the Senate has made no reservation about your claim, except for the one which, for the same religious reasons, is applicable to everyone.

There the matter rested for the time being. Cicero, feeling that Lentulus was owed some explanation, wrote a long rhetorical letter with only this consolation to offer:

168.

CICERO *ad Fam.* 1.7 [Rome, late August 56, to Lentulus Spinther] (4) At least there is no senatorial decree actually debarring you from restoring the king of Alexandria; the measure drafted to the effect that no one at all should restore the king was, as you know, vetoed; it carried so little weight that it looked more like the whim of a few angry men than the agreed policy of the Senate. So you can see what action and attainments are within your grasp as governor of Cilicia and Cyprus.

THE TRIAL OF MILO

Pompey's loss of popularity was most clearly shown when in February he tried to defend Milo against Clodius and was shouted down by the crowd (cf. no. **167**). Even the Senate, whose champion he had been a few months before, seemed to have turned against him.

The trial of Milo, postponed from Feb. 2nd, took place on the 6th.

169.

CICERO *ad Q.f.* 2.3 [Rome, 12 Feb. 56] (2) Pompey spoke, or rather tried to; for, as soon as he got to his feet, Clodius' gangs raised a great hullabaloo. He had to put up with this sort of interruption through the whole of his speech — and it wasn't just shouting, but abuse and insults as well. . . . When he had finished, up got Clodius, to be met by such an uproar from our side (we thought it only right to return the favour) that he lost all composure and self-control . . . Finally, pale with fury, he made himself heard above the din, and asked his supporters 'Who is it who is letting the people starve to death?' 'Pompey' came the answer. 'Who wants to go to Alexandria?' 'Pompey.' 'Whom do you want to go?' 'Crassus' they replied. Crassus was actually there at the time, but showed no great sympathy for Milo.

Similar abuse is recorded in Plutarch's account (*Pomp.* 48.7).

The Senate met on Feb. 8th and declared that the events of Milo's trial (which had ended in uproar and again been postponed to the 17th) had been contrary to the interests of the state.

170.

CICERO *ad Q.f.* 2.3 [Rome, 12 Feb. 56] (3) On that day Cato launched a violent attack on Pompey and throughout his speech laid charges against him as if he were actually in the dock . . . Pompey replied in equally violent terms and made pointed allusions to Crassus, saying openly 'I shall take more care to protect my life than Africanus did against his murderer, C. Carbo.' (4) So it looks to me as if important issues are developing . . . Pompey realizes that there is a conspiracy afoot threatening his life; he has also told me that Cato is being sponsored by Crassus and that Clodius has got financial backing too. Apart from Crassus, other opponents of his, such as Curio and Bibulus, are giving their support to the agitators ... So he is taking steps and collecting men from the country districts, while Clodius also reinforces his gangs.

> Scipio Africanus died under mysterious circumstances in 129; Carbo was one of many suspects, but nothing was ever proved.

171.

CICERO *ad Q.f.* 2.4 [Rome, March 56] (5) Caninius' proposal about Pompey is no longer a burning issue. Truth to tell, it has never been popular; Pompey is criticized for ingratitude to Lentulus and is really a shadow of his proper self. His patronage of Milo gives some offence to the degraded dregs of the populace, while the *optimates* find as much fault with what he does as what he fails to do.

> This is how Cicero accounts for Pompey's fall from favour. Is it a full enough explanation? What for instance did Pompey do or fail to do that dissatisfied the *optimates*?

B. The Conference of Luca

OPPOSITION TO CAESAR

The campaign of 57 ended with the complete pacification of the Belgic tribes of northern Gaul. The effect of this prestigious victory was to resolve the doubts of many other states about the advisability of further resistance. By the time winter came, Caesar could feel that his Gallic mission was complete and that he could look again at the Illyrian situation (see nos. **136** ff.).

172.

CAESAR *B.G.* 2.35 (1) These achievements [see nos. **133** f.] completed the pacification of Gaul. The news of this war had such an effect on the barbarians that envoys were sent to Caesar by the peoples who lived on the other side of the Rhine, promising hostages and obedience to his commands. (2) As Caesar was in a hurry to get to Italy and Illyria, he told these envoys to come back to him at the beginning of the next summer. (3) Caesar then left for Italy ... [etc. as in no. **135**] ...

In spite of the public recognition given to his achievements, the apparent completion of his mission now gave to Caesar's enemies a chance to clamour for his recall.

173.

DIO 39.25 (1) Pompey was deeply resentful of Caesar's increasing success; he was hurt by the people's admiration for Caesar's achievements, which made them send a senatorial commission, as if to take charge of a completely conquered Gaul, and pin such hopes on him that they voted him large sums of money. (2) In fact he tried to persuade the consuls not to read out Caesar's despatches straightaway, but keep them out of the way for as long as possible, until his achievements advertised themselves; he even wanted to send out a successor before his command officially ended.

The elections for the year 56 provided some indication of the waning of Caesar's influence at Rome; no less so the fact that Cicero, in his defence of Publius Sestius (see nos. 149 ff.), could launch a full-scale attack on Vatinius who had supplied most of the evidence for the prosecution (for Vatinius' tribunate, see no. 72).

174.

CICERO *Vat.* 38. You have managed to convince yourself that no opposition of god or man will prevent you getting everything you want, thanks to the unbelievable affection that Caesar holds for you; but have you never heard, has no one ever told you what Caesar said recently at Aquileia when various people were being discussed [cf. no. 139]? He admitted to being greatly annoyed that C. Alfius had been passed over [? for the praetorship], as he knew him to be a man of great loyalty and integrity; he was also angry at the election to the praetorship of a man [Domitius Calvinus] who disagreed with his policies. Then when someone asked him how he reacted to the news about Vatinius, he replied that Vatinius had done nothing in his tribunate without payment, and so a man for whom money was everything ought not to mind failing to win office [the aedileship].

In the Senate Caesar's legislation of 59 about the Campanian land (see nos. 18 ff.) came under attack. The discussion was opened at the end of 57, but was adjourned because of Pompey's absence (Cic. *ad Q.f.* 2.1.1, Dec. 57) until the following spring. In March the consul Lentulus prevented Gaius Cato from passing some 'monstrous proposals' about Caesar (it is not known what these were; see Cic. *ad Q.f.* 2.4.5), and in April Pompey returned.

175.
CICERO *ad Q.f.* 2.5 [Rome, 11 April 56] (1) On April 5th the Senate passed a decree giving Pompey up to 40,000,000 sesterces for the corn-supply. But on the same day there was a heated debate about the Campanian land, in which the Senate became as rowdy as an open-air meeting. The shortage of money and the high price of corn made the discussion more embittered.

176.
CICERO *ad Q.f.* 2.6 [Rome, May 56] (1) On May 15th there was a good attendance at the Senate . . . (2) The question of the Campanian land which was supposed to have been dealt with on the 15th and 16th was never in fact dealt with. But I can't go into that now.

The reason for the suspension of the debate was probably connected with the calling of the conference of Luca (see nos. **178** ff.). What is harder to determine is Cicero's part in the proceedings. In a letter written two and a half years later he set out a long and elaborate defence of his political conduct in 56, particularly of his change of sides. Since the events there described were not contemporary, and since Cicero was pleading a special case, the reliability of the letter as a historical source is impaired. Even the style is rhetorical, and the evidence he cites should be regarded in the same sort of light as that produced in his public speeches.

177.
CICERO *ad Fam.* 1.9 [Rome, Dec. 54, to Publius Lentulus] (8) [Cicero has just recalled the strong anti-Caesarian line he had taken even in Feb. 56, when in his defence of Sestius he had attacked the tribunate of Vatinius] . . . And what is more, on April 5th in the same year the Senate accepted my proposal that a full meeting of the House be held on May 15th to deal with the question of the Campanian land. Could I have launched a more determined attack on the triumvirs' citadel? Could I have shown a greater disregard for my present situation or a better recollection of my glorious past? This declaration of mine caused a great stir not only among people who were bound to react so, but others too whom I would

D

never have expected. (9) When the Senate had passed a decree on the lines of my proposal, Pompey, without showing any signs of offence, set out for Sardinia and Africa; on the way he met Caesar at Luca. There Caesar, who had already seen Crassus at Ravenna and by him been incited against me, raised many objections to my proposal. Of course it was generally known that Pompey was annoyed by it; apart from what others told me, I had the clearest information from my brother. When Pompey met him in Sardinia, a few days after leaving Luca, he said 'Ah, just the man I was looking for. What a happy coincidence! You'd better have serious words with your brother Marcus, or you'll forfeit the pledge you made to me on behalf of his conduct.'

> Does this account tally with the other evidence? If not, why would Cicero have invented it? See nos. 183 ff. for his behaviour after Luca.

THE CONFERENCE OF LUCA

Caesar responded to the political situation by reopening negotiations with his partners. His immediate need was to keep the belligerent Domitius out of the consulship, but there were other long-term provisions to make about commands and magistracies. How much was agreed at the time we can only conjecture from the variant accounts of the meeting. (For detailed discussion, see Bibliography.)

178.

SUETONIUS *Div. Jul.* 24 (1) When Lucius Domitius declared his candidature for the consulship and publicly threatened to do as consul what he had been unable to as praetor — to deprive Caesar of his army — Crassus and Pompey were summoned to Luca, a city in Caesar's province He then prevailed on them to bar Domitius from the consulship by standing themselves. He also saw to it that, with their help, his command was extended for a further five years.

179.

APPIAN *B.C.* 2.17 (62) From there [Cisalpine Gaul] Caesar distributed large sums of money to numerous people in Rome and kept in touch with the annual magistrates and other distinguished men on their way out to provincial and military commands. In fact there were at one time 120 lictors in his presence, and two hundred or more Senators, some returning thanks for services already rendered, some trying to make money, some to secure their advancement in other ways. Caesar's great army, affluence and readiness to bestow favours meant that he controlled everything. (63) Among those who came to see him were Pompey and Crassus, his partners in power. As a result of their deliberations, it was decided that Pompey and Crassus should be re-elected consuls and that Caesar should have his provincial command extended for a further five years.

Plutarch's account is very similar, prefaced also by mention of Caesar's widespread bribery and his meeting with the 200 senators. (Plut. *Caes.* 21.1–2).

180.

PLUTARCH *Pomp.* 51. (1) Meanwhile Caesar had achieved a great reputation as a result of his Gallic wars; but although he seemed to be a very long way from Rome and tied up with the Belgians, Suebi, and Britons, yet his cleverness enabled him to counteract Pompey's political designs, in the very heart of the city when it really mattered, without Pompey knowing . . . (4) [After his meeting with the Senators at Luca] when all the others had been sent away with their pockets full and their hopes high, he came to an arrangement with Pompey and Crassus: they were to stand jointly for the consulship, and he would assist at the election by sending a large body of soldiers; as soon as they were elected, they were to secure provincial commands and armies for themselves and see to it that his command was guaranteed for another five years.

181.

PLUTARCH *Crass.* 14 (4) Pompey's part was motivated by his insatiable desire for power; but Crassus had fallen victim to another disease beside his chronic avarice — the brilliant victories of Caesar made him envious of the trophies and triumphs which were the one thing lacking to make his superiority over Caesar complete.

In Dio's account, prefaced by a description of Pompey's increasing jealousy of Caesar (see no. **173**), the emphasis is quite different and there is no mention of Caesar at all in the negotiations.

182.

DIO 39.26 (3) For reasons of this kind Pompey began arming himself against Caesar. As he did not think he could succeed on his own, he attached himself even more closely to Crassus, so that Caesar could be overthrown with his help. 27 (1) After conferring, they agreed that private citizenship limited their prospects, but that consulship would give them control of affairs to rival Caesar's: there would not just be a balance of power, but, as two against one, they would quickly outweigh him. (2) So now they laid aside the pretence of no longer wanting the consulship (a pretence which they had put up whenever one of their associates had urged them to compete for the office); now they set all their sights on it, even though they had just been campaigning on behalf of other candidates.

The excerpts quoted (nos. **172–82**) suggest at any rate three different versions of the negotiations which led to the settlement described below: that Caesar acted entirely on his own initiative (Appian and Plutarch); that he was reacting to the pressure of the *optimates* (Suetonius and perhaps Cicero); or that his hand was forced by Pompey and Crassus (Dio). Is there any way of choosing between the different explanations?

RESULTS OF THE LUCA CONFERENCE

The most important immediate result of the conference was the recantation of Cicero, who was persuaded of the folly of continued opposition to the partnership. His change of sides was demonstrated publicly by his delivering in June or July 56 the speech 'On the Consular Provinces'; this recommended that Caesar should be given more money and allowed to stay in Gaul for the last two years of his allotted command so that he could finish the task of conquest (cf. no. **102**). Once that had been accepted, it only remained for Domitius to be excluded from the consulship in favour of Pompey and Crassus, and Caesar could regard his position as safe once more. Then finally plans could be made for the allocation of the provincial commands for 54 (see nos. **195** ff., esp. **197** n.).

183.

CICERO *ad Att.* 4.5 [Antium, April or May 56] (1) I confess my 'palinode' does look rather shameful. But goodbye to honesty, truth and honour in politics! . . . (2) I tell you, I wanted to bind myself to this alliance and remove any opportunity of drifting back to the people, whose jealousy of me never ends, even when they should be pitying me . . . Enough. Since I am refused affection by the powerless, I shall do my best to win it from the powerful.

> This 'palinode' was probably the speech 'On the Consular Provinces' which he was already preparing.

184.
CICERO *Prov. Cos.* 28. We have recently had put before us a proposal about pay for Caesar's army; I not only voted for it, but did my best to see that you voted for it too; I countered a number of objections; I was a member of the drafting committee.

185.
CICERO *Prov. Cos.* 34. One or two summers can bind the whole of Gaul to us with everlasting chains, through hope or fear, punishment or rewards, weapons or laws. But if the situation is left unresolved, without the finishing touches, then, however much cut back, those people will break out again and reopen the war with fresh vigour. . . . 35. Caesar has now done enough to satisfy his own requirements, but not those of the state; and since he is prepared to wait to enjoy the fruits of his labours rather than give up his state office half-completed, we should not upset things by recalling a general who is set on serving the state well, nor interrupt the unfolding of a comprehensive Gallic policy which is already near completion.

186.
CICERO *Balb.* 61. The Senate has honoured Caesar with a public thanksgiving of the most generous kind and of unprecedented length [see no. 135]. It has also provided pay for his victorious army in spite of the shortage of public funds, decreed that he as general should have ten legates and should not be superseded under the terms of the Sempronian law. I was the author and prime mover of these proposals; for I thought it better to promote unity as the present situation demands, than to follow my earlier principles of antagonism.

This speech was delivered a month or two later in defence of L. Cornelius Balbus, one of Caesar's agents in Rome, who was charged with usurping citizenship. It is significant that both Pompey and Crassus spoke on his behalf as well (Cic. *Balb.* 17).

For the Sempronian Law, see no. **71** intro.

That Cicero still had some private misgivings about this change of sides is apparent from his letters:

187.

CICERO *ad Fam.* 1.7 [Rome, late August 56, to Lentulus Spinther] (10) You tell me you want to know about the political situation. There is plenty of disagreement, but the fight is one-sided. The people with all the big guns and resources seem to me to have profited so much from the dithering ineptitude of their opponents that now they carry greater authority as well. So, with only a handful of dissentients, they have managed to get through the Senate things which they did not expect to obtain even through the people, except by violent methods; Caesar has had pay voted him, and ten legates, and has had no trouble in preventing a successor being sent out under the Sempronian law. I am not going to write in detail about this, because the situation gives me no pleasure; but I just write to give you this advice . . . never sacrifice dignity for the sake of safety, or safety for the sake of dignity.

By the time Pompey and Crassus announced their candidature for the consulship, the legal closing-date had passed. As the consul Gnaius Marcellinus refused to make an exception in their favour, they had to engineer a postponement till the following year (Dio 39.30.3). Domitius knew that he had no chance, but continued to compete even so, until physical intimidation was finally used to deter him.

188.

DIO 39.27 (3) Pompey and Crassus began canvassing outside the period laid down by the law, but when a number of people including the consuls (for Marcellinus was not without influence) made it clear that they would prevent the election, they used the assistance of Gaius Cato and others to ensure that the elections should not take place during the current year; this would necessitate the appointment of an *interrex* which would make their candidature and election legal.

189.

CICERO *ad Att.* 4.8b [?Tusculum, ? autumn 56] (2) As for Domitius, his case is just like mine — the same people responsible, the same unexpectedness, the same desertion by the *optimates*. The only difference is that he deserved it. But perhaps his fate is harder to bear: he was marked out for the consulship ever since he was born and then failed to get it, even though there was not more than one candidate in the field against him. It may be true that Pompey has on the pages of his note-book lists of as many consuls as ex-consuls; if that is so, Domitius' plight is only rivalled by that of the country, where even hopes for a better future are impossible.

> Compare the sentiments expressed by Cicero in these letters (nos. **183, 187, 189**) with what he says in his speeches (nos. **184–6**).

190.

DIO 39.31 (1) In due course Pompey and Crassus were elected consuls following an interregnum, as there was no opposition from those who had earlier announced their candidature. In fact Lucius Domitius did continue his campaign until the last day; but when he left home that evening to go to the assembly, the boy carrying the light in front of him was murdered. This frightened him so much that he proceeded no further. (2) So there was no opposition, and in any case the arrival in Rome of an army under Publius Crassus (son of Marcus, and at that time one of Caesar's officers) ensured that there was no difficulty about their election.

191.

PLUTARCH *Pomp.* 52 (1) Although the other candidates for the consulship gave up their electoral campaigns, yet Cato persuaded and encouraged Lucius Domitius to persevere; the fight, he said, was not for office, but for freedom in the face of tyranny. Pompey's supporters were afraid that Cato's resoluteness might, with the support of the whole Senate, change the minds even of the dependable elements among the people and win them to his side; (2) so, to prevent Domitius going down to the forum, they sent an armed gang which killed the torch-bearer at the head of the party and put the rest to flight. Cato was the last to retire, after being wounded in the right arm while fighting in defence of Domitius.

V. The Consulship of Pompey and Crassus

The Conference of Luca had saved Caesar from the immediate threat of recall. By giving the appearance of presenting a united front, he and his partners had intimidated the active opposition and persuaded the leading senatorial spokesman, Cicero, to plead on their own behalf. This did not mean that the balance of the partnership was restored as well and that the situation in 55 would be the same as in 58. If anything, Caesar had had to concede ground in order to ensure that his cause at Rome did not suffer irreparably. He had obtained an assurance that he would not be superseded before the end of his command and had probably discussed his future plans for Gaul which justified his spending a further five years there; but entrusting the necessary legislation to his two potential rivals was a very different matter from using a co-operative tribune. He could not promote his own interests without allowing them to do the same, and this increased the chances of an effective coalition being formed against him.

Pompey and Crassus may have been satisfied initially just with the prestige of holding office again; they certainly made little use of the opportunity to pass significant legislation, except to secure for themselves large provincial commands which would theoretically put them on a military par with Caesar. Crassus appears to have had ideas of emulating Caesar's Gallic conquests with a grandiose eastern campaign; Pompey was content to stay in Italy and allow his province to be run for him by subordinates. Whether deliberately or not, he was thus left in a position to dictate the course of politics at Rome, if the situation and his own inclinations suggested it.

The behaviour of his partners would bring little comfort to Caesar, as it was not difficult to imagine that both were motivated by a desire to increase personal influence and prestige at his expense. For Caesar therefore it was essential to strengthen his alliances at Rome and to enhance his public reputation with another striking military triumph, such as the conquest of Britain.

The year 55 brings all the leading political characters into prominence, and the sources used in this chapter give an idea of the relative progress they make towards their different objectives.

A. The consulship of Pompey and Crassus

THE ELECTIONS FOR 55

To save themselves the trouble of having to fight for their legislation, it was important for Pompey and Crassus that the elections for the other magistracies, also held over from the previous year, should be carefully controlled.

192.

PLUTARCH *Cat. Min.* 42 (1) So Pompey and Crassus were elected consuls, but Cato would still not give up. He next put himself forward as a candidate for the praetorship so that he would have a good base for his campaign against them, and would not have to take his stand as a private citizen facing magistrates. They in turn had similar fears: that in his hands the praetorship would rival the consulship. (2) Their first move was to call a sudden surprise meeting of the Senate, where it was voted that praetors should take up office immediately after election, without leaving the statutory time-gap in which cases against those who had bribed the people could be heard. Then, after this decree had removed the sanctions upon bribery, they brought forward as candidates for the praetorship clients and friends of their own, and not only distributed bribes but stood watching as the votes were cast. (3) However even that could not neutralize Cato's goodness and reputation: shame made people see the iniquity of betraying him with their votes when it was fair that the city should buy him as praetor. So the first tribe to be called upon cast their votes for him. In a moment Pompey dissolved the assembly, declaring with scandalous dishonesty that he had heard thunder . . . (4) By liberal use of bribery a second time and by the ejection of the *optimates* from the Campus Martius, they forcibly carried through the election of Vatinius instead of Cato as praetor.

> The presiding magistrate could bring electoral proceedings to a halt by announcing an unfavourable omen such as thunder. This was a power easily and not infrequently abused (cf. nos. **160** f.).

193.

CICERO *ad Q.f.* 2.7 [Rome, Feb. 55] (3) On Feb. 11th the Senate fiassed a decree about bribery along the lines of Afranius' proposal which I told you about when you were here. But they showed their disapproval when the consuls paid no attention to the suggestion that, while accepting Afranius' proposal, they should add a rider ensuring that a praetor remained a private citizen for two months after election. On that day Cato suffered an open rebuff. What more is there to say? They hold all the strings and want everyone to know it.

194.

DIO 39.32 (3) As they themselves held the elections, they appointed magistrates to suit their own interests, and befriended the aediles and most of the tribunes, who were elected by the people. There were however two tribunes, Gaius Ateius Capito and Publius Aquilius Gallus, who did not go along with them.

PROVINCIAL COMMANDS

At the end of the year Pompey emerged with a five-year command in Spain, Crassus a similar one in Syria, and Caesar's in Gaul had been extended for a further five years. But there is some disagreement in the sources over the manner in which this came about. There are suggestions that the consular provinces were assigned by lot, not choice; that Caesar's supporters in Rome were unhappy about his partners' influence, and that the extension of his command was only added later as a concession.

195.

PLUTARCH *Cat. Min.* 43 (1) Gaius Trebonius proposed a law about the distribution of provinces to the consuls; one was to have Spain and Libya, the other Syria and Egypt, with the power to make war on any they chose and use naval and military forces to overpower them. Most people had given up the idea of trying to oppose or prevent them and did not even raise a voice in protest; but Cato got up on the platform before the vote was taken, and was grudgingly given a limit of two hours in which to speak. [At the end of this time he had to be forcibly removed, but did his best to get back] . . . (3) After this had happened a number of times, Trebonius gave orders for him to be taken off to prison. But a crowd accompanied him as he went, listening to what he said, and Trebonius was frightened into letting him go.

196.

PLUTARCH *Crass.* 16 (1) When the distribution of provinces had been determined by lot, Crassus was jubilant. He acted as though this was the best piece of good fortune he had ever had; in public, even among strangers, he could hardly restrain himself, while to his friends he made any number of empty and childish boasts. This did not accord with his age, or indeed his character, which had always been quite free of swagger and bombast. (2) But now he was quite beside himself with excitement — he wouldn't imagine Syria as the limit of his successes, or even Parthia; he would make the achievements of Lucullus against Tigranes, and Pompey against Mithridates look like child's play. In fact his hopes carried him all the way to Bactria, India and the Outer Ocean. (3) Actually there had been no mention of a Parthian war in the law passed about their commands. But everyone knew that Crassus was very excited by the idea, and Caesar wrote an approving letter from Gaul encouraging him in his war-project.

> This suggests that the original bill did not assign the Syrian command specifically to Crassus. Why, when he did get it, should Caesar have been so enthusiastic about his projected campaign? What reasons might he have had for wanting to keep Crassus well out of the way?

197.

DIO 39.33 (2) The tribune Gaius Trebonius proposed that to one of the consuls should be given Syria and the neighbouring area, to the other the Spanish provinces, where there had in fact been some trouble. They were to have a five-year command, with the power to use whatever citizens and allies they wanted in their armies, and to make peace and war with anyone they chose. (3) This move was unpopular with many people, especially Caesar's friends, who felt that if the consuls got what they wanted they would be bound to restrict the growth of Caesar's power. Some of them were preparing to oppose the measure when the consuls, afraid of finding their ambitions frustrated, reconciled them by giving Caesar too an extension of command — for three years, to give the proper figure. (4) Even so they did not bring before the people any proposals on his behalf until their own position had been ratified. Caesar's friends had, as I say, been won over, and so kept quiet; most of the rest were too inhibited by fear to do anything else, happy if that would at least preserve their skins. 34 (1) But Cato and Favonius, with the assistance of the two tribunes and some others, opposed their every move. However in the face of such odds they achieved nothing by speaking out.

Is it plausible that Caesar's supporters should have objected to the bill of Trebonius if this had been part of the agreement at Luca? Or is this adequate evidence for supposing that no arrangement had ever been made with the consuls about the extension of Caesar's command? Note that Dio gives the period of this extension as three, not five years.

198.

CICERO *ad Att.* 4.9 [Cumae, 27 April 55] (1) Pompey has been here with me. He had plenty to say about the political situation and was not satisfied with himself — or so he said, a necessary qualification in his case; he showed contempt for Syria and made much of Spain — again, so he said.

The manuscript reading (*laetans* = 'gladdening') makes no sense, and *iactans* has been suggested as an alternative. However some editors have taken this to mean 'make little of' rather than the reverse which I have preferred (see *Cicero's Letters to Atticus* ed. Shackleton Bailey (C.U.P., 1965), Vol. II, pp. 101, 196).

The use that each of the consuls made of the province assigned to him makes interesting comparison; the sources are agreed about Crassus' ambition, but different reasons are given for Pompey's decision to stay near Rome:

199.

PLUTARCH *Pomp.* 52 (4) Crassus went out to his province immediately after the end of his year as consul, but Pompey stayed to open his theatre; the dedication ceremony included gymnastic and musical competitions, as well as animal fights in which 500 lions were killed before the climax of the elephant-battle — a stupendous spectacle. 53 (1) This won him admiration and affection, although the effect was neutralized by the jealousy aroused when he handed over his armies and provinces to old friends so that he could go from place to place round the popular resorts of Italy with his wife. Either he was so in love with her, or she with him, that he could not leave her.

200.

APPIAN *B.C.* 2.18 (65) Crassus chose Syria and the surrounding country as his province because he wanted a campaign against the Parthians, which he thought would bring him easy glory and profit. (66) But there were many unfavourable omens as he left the city: the tribunes forbade the campaign as the Parthians had done nothing to offend and, when Crassus paid no attention, they called public curses down on him.

201.

DIO 39.39 (1) This [sc. the games described in no. **199**] won Pompey considerable popularity, but when he started making levies with Crassus for the campaigns which had been voted to them, the people strongly resented it . . . (3) In fact the tribunes tried to stop the levies and repeal the vote for the campaigns. (4) At this Pompey was not at all put out; he had wasted no time in sending out subordinates while he remained in the country himself. He could claim that he was prevented from absenting himself for many reasons, especially because of the need to stay and look after the corn-supply. But in any case he was happy to do so, as his idea was to let his men get control of Spain, while he controlled everything in Rome and the rest of Italy himself. (5) But none of this applied to Crassus, and he looked to the force of arms. The tribunes then saw that no amount of free speech, without armed backing, could prevent his undertaking; and so they kept quiet apart from pronouncing many terrible curses on him (although cursing him entailed cursing the state). (6) In fact, when he was making the usual prayers for his campaign on the Capitol, they started spreading stories about omens and portents; and as he departed, they pronounced a number of fearsome curses on him; (7) but when the other tribunes objected, they came into conflict. In the resulting lull Crassus went outside the *pomerium*.

For some of the adverse prodigies reported, see Cic. *Div.* 2.84, Val. Max. 1.6.11.

202.

CICERO *ad Att.* 4.13 [Tusculum, late Nov. 55] (2) They tell me that when our friend Crassus set off in his uniform he made a less dignified showing than did Lucius Paullus, who matched his years and two consulships years ago. What a good for nothing he is!

> L. Aemilius Paullus was 60 when he left for Macedonia in his second consulship (168 B.C.).

The elections for the following year showed some gain by the opposition.

203.

DIO 39.60 (2) When they laid down their office, they were succeeded by Lucius Domitius and Appius Claudius ... (3) Domitius was ill-disposed towards Pompey because of the electioneering tactics which had given Pompey the office he himself wanted [see nos. **188-191**]; and Claudius, although related to Pompey, was still prepared to play the demagogue and pander to the people's wishes.

> Pompey's elder son had married one of Appius' daughters. (Cic. *ad Fam.* 3.4.2).

204.

PLUTARCH *Cat Min.* 44 (1) Cato was elected praetor for the following year, but it would appear that he degraded the office and detracted more from its dignity and importance than he added to it by good service. Often he would go off to his tribunal wearing neither shoes nor tunic, and presided over capital trials involving distinguished men, dressed as he was. Some people even say that he conducted business after drinking wine at the mid-day meal. But there is no truth in that report.

CICERO

Cicero's political activity was limited this year and he devoted more time to his writing (the three books 'On the Orator' were nearing completion in November; *ad. Att.* 4.13.2). His only recorded speeches are those against L. Piso, consul in 58 recently returned from Macedonia, and on behalf of Caninius Gallus who as tribune in 56 had supported Pompey's claims for assisting Ptolemy (see no. **171**). Even so his friendship was regarded as worth having by all the leading politicians.

205.

CICERO *ad Fam.* 1.8 [Rome, Jan. 55, to Lentulus Spinther] (1) Public affairs are all, it is true, under the control of our friends, and their grip is such that I can't see any possibility of a change during our lifetime. (2) For my own part, I am doing as I ought, as you yourself prompted me and as my sense of duty and expediency compels me, in attaching myself to the man whose attachment you prized in supporting my interests . . . I am moulding myself to his will, as it would not be right for me to break with him. This is not hypocrisy, as people might think. The dictates of my heart (including of course my affection for Pompey) mean so much to me that I am inclined to accept as right and true whatever he desires or thinks expedient, and, I would have thought, even his opponents wouldn't go far wrong if they gave up fighting such an obviously one-sided battle. (3) I am also consoled by the thought that I am the sort of person to whom everyone gives all possible deference, whether I support Pompey's wishes or hold my peace, or even, as I feel most inclined to do, return to my literary studies; that is in fact what I shall do if my friendship with Pompey permits it. When I had laid aside the exacting demands and high honours of public office, my avowed intention had been to maintain dignity in senatorial debate and freedom in public affairs. Now every hope of doing so has been destroyed, as much for everyone else as for me. Now the choice lies between undignified agreement with the minority and ineffectual opposition. (4) My main reason for writing this is to encourage you to look to your own position as well. The whole character of the Senate, the law courts and the state in general has been transformed. All I can hope is that I shall be left alone; and the holders of power look as if they will grant me that, provided that certain people show more tolerance of the régime.

206.
(For the context of this letter, see the introduction to no. **177**.)
CICERO *ad Fam.* 1.9 [Rome, Dec. 54, to Lentulus Spinther] (19) As soon as Vatinius was elected praetor, Pompey stepped in to negotiate a reconciliation between us. I had indeed vigorously attacked his candidature in the Senate, although my intention had been not so much to injure him as to defend and do honour to Cato; then followed the surprising insistence of Caesar's that I should speak in Vatinius' defence [cf. no. **243**; Cicero had in 56 attacked Vatinius at the trial of Sestius — see no. **174**.] (20) . . .

[Cicero now talks of his relations with Crassus, and, how delighted people were when they disagreed over the treatment of Gabinius — see nos. 244 ff.] . . . When these scandalous remarks were reported to me by men of irreproachable character, when Pompey had tried as never before to reconcile Crassus and me again, when Caesar showed in his letters how strongly he disapproved of our estrangement — then I took into consideration not only the current situation, but my natural inclinations as well; so, to give the Roman people indisputable evidence of our reconciliation, Crassus actually set out to his province from just about under my roof. For he came to dine with me in the country house of my son-in-law Crassipes.

207.

PLUTARCH *Cic.* 26 (1) Crassus decided that he would prefer to have Cicero as a friend than an enemy; so, just before he departed for Syria, he said in a friendly spirit that he would like to dine with him; and Cicero was very ready to entertain him.

208.

CICERO *ad Fam.* 5.8 [Rome, Jan. 54, to M. Licinius Crassus on his way to Syria] (1) The ardour I showed in defending, I might almost say increasing, the honour of your position will, I am sure, have been described in the letters of your friends. There was nothing half-hearted about it; it wasn't the sort of thing you could fail to observe, or pass over in silence. I took up my stand against the consuls and a number of ex-consuls, and showed more fighting spirit than I have ever done in any other case. I took upon myself the permanent task of championing your illustrious name and discharged in full the debt owed for some time to our long-standing friendship, interrupted though it has been by the constantly changing times.

The consular attack may have been about Crassus' expenses. Compare Cicero's sentiments here with those in no. 202.

B. *Caesar's campaigns in 56/55*

THE VENETI

When Caesar left the Conference at Luca, he still had two campaigning seasons to go before his original command expired at the end of Feb. 54

(Cic. *Prov. Cos.* 37). New ground for conquest was essential if he was to maintain his prestige, and yet he claimed that Gaul was completely pacified (see nos. **135, 172**). He had apparently already decided against an Illyrian campaign (see nos. **137** ff.) and was perhaps already looking towards either Britain or Germany. If so, some apprehension among the tribes most immediately affected would be understandable. The Veneti were the strongest of the tribes on the north Atlantic coast, and, though Caesar takes particular trouble to justify his hostilities against them, it is equally possible that he picked a quarrel, or that they were trying to forestall his attempt on Britain since they knew that it would interfere with their own advantageous position (cf. no. **223**).

209.

CAESAR *B.G.* 3.7 (1) Suddenly the war started up in Gaul, and this was the reason. (2) The young Publius Crassus had spent the winter among the Andes on the Atlantic coast (see no. **134**). (3) As there was a food shortage in the area, he sent some of his senior officers and military tribunes into the neighbouring states in search of supplies; (4) among these was . . . Quintus Velanius, who with Titus Silius went to the Veneti. 8 (1) These Veneti are much the most important of all the maritime states in the area, as they have the largest number of ships (in which they regularly sail to Britain) and the greatest skill and experience in nautical matters; besides, they control the few harbours which exist as shelter from the danger of the open sea and so exact tolls from almost all those who regularly sail on it. (2) It was these people who first arrested Silius and Velanius, hoping to be able to exchange them for the hostages which they had given to Crassus . . . (5) This led to similar action by the other maritime states, and a combined embassy was sent to Crassus to demand the return of their hostages. . . . 9 (1) Crassus passed this news on to Caesar; as Caesar was still some way away, he ordered that the time he took to arrive should be spent building warships on the Loire (which flows into the Ocean), conscripting rowers in the Province and collecting mariners and pilots. (2) These orders were quickly seen to, and Caesar set out to join his army as soon as the weather allowed him. (3) When the Veneti and the other states learned of Caesar's arrival, they took steps to make war-preparations on the scale demanded by the gravity of the situation; for they realized how serious their offence had been in arresting and imprisoning envoys, whose status had always been regarded as inviolate and universally sacrosanct.

210.

CAESAR *B.G.* 3.10 (1) There were many factors that gave urgency to Caesar's war-preparations: (2) the insult of Roman Knights being arrested, the rebellion coming after surrender, the defection after giving hostages, the number of states involved in the conspiracy, above all the fear that if he did nothing about this area other peoples would consider themselves entitled to follow their example.

To prevent the possibility of a general uprising, Caesar distributed his troops widely over Gaul.

211.

CAESAR *B.G.* 3.11 (1) He sent Titus Labienus as general with some cavalry into the territory of the Treveri who live beside the Rhine. (2) His orders were to secure the continued loyalty of the Remi and the Belgian tribes by his presence and to prevent any forcible attempts being made to sail across the river by the Germans who were said to have been invited to help them. (3) He ordered Publius Crassus to make for Aquitania with twelve legionary cohorts and a large cavalry detachment, to prevent help being sent to Gaul from this area and the possibility of a powerful coalition. (4) Quintus Titurius Sabinus was sent, with three legions under his command, into the territory of the Venelli, Curiosolites, and Lexovii, to keep that area segregated. (5) The young Decius Brutus was put in charge of the fleet together with the Gallic ships which had been commandeered from the Pictones, Santones, and other pacified tribes; his orders were to head for the Veneti country with all speed, while Caesar himself brought up the infantry forces.

After capturing a number of enemy strongholds, Caesar realized that the only way to defeat the Veneti was by naval confrontation. So he brought his ships into action and, by means of a grappling device which cut the enemy's rigging, won a comprehensive victory.

212.

CAESAR *B.G.* 3.16 (1) This battle brought to an end the war with the Veneti and the whole of the maritime coast, (2) the reason being that they had assembled in one place all the younger men and such of their elders as had any ideas or importance, together with all the ships anywhere available. (3) After losing them, they had no refuge left them and no means of defending their towns. So they gave themselves up to Caesar with all their possessions.

At the same time Crassus carried out a successful campaign in Aquitania, compelling all but the remotest tribes to surrender. (*B.G.* 3.20–27).

213.

CAESAR *B.G.* 3.28 (1) At about the same time, even though the summer was almost over, Caesar led an army against the Menapii and Morini, as, when all the rest of Gaul was pacified, they alone remained under arms and had never sent representatives to negotiate peace with him.

> This does not seem a very strong pretext, and suspicions of an ulterior motive may be aroused by the fact that the Menapii and Morini occupied the part of the coast commanding the shortest crossing to Britain (for similar doubts about Caesar's integrity, see no. **255** n.). In fact Caesar did not win outright victory, but after widespread depredations brought his troops back into winter-quarters among the recently defeated tribes.

THE USIPETES AND TENCTERI

Much of the next campaigning season (55) was taken up with punitive measures against two German tribes which had crossed the Rhine. From this Caesar derived little credit or satisfaction, and his ruthlessness may reflect his impatience at being diverted from the British project. It is quite likely, as some of the sources suggest, that his subsequent crossing of the Rhine was intended to offset the unpopularity of his action against the Germans.

214.

CAESAR *B.G.* 4.1 (1) In the following winter, which marked the beginning of the year when Pompey and Crassus were consuls, two German tribes, the Usipetes and Tencteri, crossed the Rhine in enormous numbers not far from where the river joins the sea. (2) The reason for their migration was the pressure exerted on them by the Suebi, who had been harassing them for some years and preventing them tilling the fields.

The Germans said that they were looking for land to settle on; Caesar replied that he had none to spare but that the Ubii might be prepared to give them some in return for assistance against the Suebi (*B.G.* 4.4–8). While the Germans opened negotiations with the Ubii, Caesar moved his camp nearer until the cavalry came within range. At once the Germans engaged with their own cavalry, and Caesar retaliated by making a surprise attack on their camp, in which he claimed that he destroyed most of their 430,000 without losing a man (*B.G.* 4.9–15). It is impossible to decide whether the Germans deserved their fate, as we have no evidence independent of Caesar. He was anxious to justify himself, particularly as his opponents in Rome made considerable capital out of the incident, and his account reflects this preoccupation: he is throughout insistent upon the treachery and duplicity of the Germans (see esp. *B.G.* 4.13), and implies that they brought retribution on themselves by their impetuous attack on the Roman cavalry.

215.

PLUTARCH *Caes.* 22 (2) About the battle which he fought with the Usipes and Tenteritae, Caesar says in his Commentaries that the barbarians attacked him on the road while still negotiating under a truce and, as his 5,000 cavalry were caught by surprise, they were put to flight by the enemy's 800; then when another deputation was sent to hoodwink him again, he detained them and led his army against the barbarians as he considered it mere folly to keep faith with such unprincipled truce-breakers. (3) But Tanusius says that when the Senate voted to celebrate the victory with festivities and sacrifices, Cato publicly declared that Caesar ought to be handed over to the barbarians, so that the city should be purged of the stigma of breaking a truce and the curse be directed against the man who was responsible.

Tanusius Geminus: an historian also mentioned in Suet. *Div. Jul.* 9.

216.

PLUTARCH *Cat. Min.* 51 (2) This [sc. Cato's attack] prompted Caesar to write a letter and send it to the Senate, full of denunciations and accusations against Cato. When it had been read out, (3) Cato stood up and, with the appearance of being deliberately prepared rather than angrily antagonistic, showed that the charges made against him were nothing more than abusive taunts, a piece of childish vulgarity on Caesar's part. Then he attacked Caesar's plans from the outset and, in the role rather of a fellow-conspirator than an enemy, revealed the whole of his designs: he said that, if they had any sense, they would be more afraid of Caesar himself than of any sons of Germans or Gauls. (4) This pointed attack struck home so forcibly that Caesar's friends regretted having the letter read in the Senate and giving Cato the opportunity to make his fair and incriminating assertions.

217.

SUETONIUS *Div. Jul.* 24 (3) After that [sc. the renewal of his command], he lost no opportunity of making war, however iniquitous or dangerous it might be — he deliberately attacked allied states as well as barbarous and hostile peoples. In the end the Senate decreed that representatives should be sent to examine the state of the Gallic provinces, and some people even declared that he ought to be handed over to the enemy.

> In fact the decree extending Caesar's command was not passed until after the German campaign.

The crossing of the Rhine.

218.

CAESAR *B.G.* 4.16 (1) Of the many reasons for deciding to cross the Rhine, the most straightforward was that the Germans were always ready to come over into Gaul, and he wanted to give them reason to think of their own safety by showing them that a Roman army was not afraid or unable to cross the Rhine.
[A second reason was that the main body of the German cavalry, which had not returned in time for the recent battle, had taken refuge with the Sugambri who now refused to give them up when Caesar demanded surrender (ch. 16.2–4). The third reason was that the Ubii had asked for his help against the Suebi (ch. 16.5–7).]

After crossing the Rhine, Caesar received various peaceful deputations, ravaged the Sugambri territory and promised help to the Ubii. Then, hearing that the Suebi were massing troops, he returned to Gaul, considering that 'he had achieved enough to satisfy his honour and his requirements' (*B.G.* 4.19.4).

Dio and Plutarch (*Caes.* 22.4) preserve a more hostile account:

219.

DIO 39.48 (3) [After the German cavalry had taken refuge with the Sugambri,] Caesar sent a demand for their surrender; it wasn't that he expected them to be given up (for the people beyond the Rhine were not so frightened by the Romans as to pay any attention to demands like that), but it would provide him with an excuse for crossing that particular river. (4) For he had a strong desire to do what none of his predecessors had ever done. He also hoped to keep the Germans at a distance away from Gaul by invading their territory himself.

At any rate some people in Rome were prepared to be impressed.

220.

CICERO *Pis.* 81. Even if Caesar had never been my friend; if he had always been bad-tempered and scornful of my friendship; if he had made himself quite unapproachable and implacable — yet even then I could not help feeling friendly towards a man whose daily achievements have been, and still are, on such a grand scale.

This speech was delivered in Sept. 55.

THE FIRST EXPEDITION TO BRITAIN

Caesar's expedition to Britain in the autumn of 55 raises two main questions: why he started so dangerously late in the year, and what the purpose of his mission was. The second question is answered, not very satisfactorily, by Caesar, and some alternative suggestions are offered by other sources. The first is more speculative; if it is felt that Caesar would not normally have taken such a desperate military risk, then it must be supposed that he was under pressure, and if he was under pressure, it must have been as a result of political events in Rome.

221.

CAESAR *B.G.* 4.20 (1) There was only a small part of the summer left, as winter comes early in all that region of Gaul which faces north. Even so Caesar set about launching an expedition to Britain. His reasons were these: he had discovered that in almost all the Gallic wars help had been sent to the enemies of Rome from that country (cf. no. **222**); (2) again, even if there was not enough time

hat year for undertaking a proper campaign, he still thought it
would be very useful just to visit the island, take a good look at the
inhabitants and collect information about the terrain, harbours, and
landing-places. The Gauls knew almost nothing about these
points.

In spite of what Caesar says above, these are the only instances of British
aid that he mentions elsewhere.

222a.
Diviciacus' plea on behalf of the rebellious Bellovaci in 57; cf. nos.
(32 f.):
CAESAR *B.G.* 2.14 (3) 'The men who were responsible for this
policy realized how disastrous it had been for their state and have
led to Britain.'

222b.
The preparations of the Veneti in 56; cf. nos. **209** ff.).
CAESAR *B.G.* 3.9 (9) For the forthcoming campaign they secured
he alliance of the Osismi, Lexovii, Namnetes, Morini, Diablintes,
and Menapii; they also sent for help from Britain, which is
situated opposite that part of the country.

Caesar's second aim was reconnaissance. It did not need a full-scale
expedition to discover suitable landing-places; he could *hope* to find out
that from merchants (even though they disappointed him), or from a
single ship sent specifically to reconnoitre (that was the mission of
Volusenus; *B.G.* 4.21.1,9). So in sending two legions and a fleet to
Britain, Caesar must have intended to penetrate deeper into the country
and discover something about the hinterland; or he must have had some
purpose other than reconnaissance in mind.

223.
STRABO 4.4 (1) It was the Veneti who fought a sea battle against
Caesar; for they were prepared to obstruct his passage to Britain,
as they made use of the British market.

This commercial link helps to explain why the Gallic states on the north
coast should want to keep independent of Caesar. It also suggests a
reason why the merchants whom Caesar asked for information about
Britain were so unhelpful; *B.G.* 4.20.4.

224.

CAESAR *B.G.* 5.12 (2) The coast of Britain is inhabited by people who have crossed over from Belgium on raids and plundering forays. Most of them settled down there after making their raids and began cultivating the land, retaining for their new states the names of the ones they had originally left in Belgium [e.g. the Atrebates, whose capital was at Silchester].

In fact the expedition not only failed to achieve anything positive but was very nearly disastrous: the cavalry transports were held up, the ships were the wrong design for landing in shallow waters, they were surprised by high tides and bad weather, and the Seventh Legion was nearly destroyed on a foraging expedition (*B.G.* 4.23–27). Nor did the expedition seem to make much impression on the British chieftains. They disregarded a truce and were negligent about sending hostages (*B.G.* 4.30–31). When Caesar returned to Gaul and ordered the defeated tribes to send him double the number of hostages (*B.G.* 4.36.2), only two bothered to do so (*B.G.* 4.38.4). And yet in spite of the near disasters, his achievement was acknowledged in Rome by a decree of twenty days' thanks-giving. This can only be understood by reference to the current state of knowledge about Britain.

225.

DIO 39.50 (2) This country [Britain] is about sixty miles away from the Belgian mainland, actually the territory of the Morini, at its nearest point. It extends along the rest of the Gallic coast and nearly the whole length of Spain, projecting well out into the sea. (3) The earliest Greeks and Romans did not know of its existence and even succeeding generations have come into conflict over whether it was an island or part of a continent. Much has been written on both sides by men who knew nothing about it.

226.

STRABO 4.5 (2) Most of the island is flat and covered with forests, although there are a number of hilly districts. It produces grain and cattle, gold, silver, and iron. These, as you would expect, are exported from the island, along with hides, slaves, and dogs which are well-built for hunting.

227.

APPIAN *Celt.* 1.5. Caesar also crossed over to Britain, an island that is larger than a very large continent and was still unknown to people in Rome at that time.

228.

FLORUS 1.45 (17) [When Caesar landed the first time . . .]. The shores were filled with disorganized enemy, hurrying this way and that in their chariots and full of alarm at the sight of this new phenomenon. This alarm served Caesar as a victory.

229.

PLUTARCH *Caes*. 23 (2) The campaign against the Britons won him great renown for his daring; for he was the first person to launch an expedition on the Western Ocean and sail over the Atlantic to fight with his army. The size of the island was unbelievable and was the subject of many disputes between different writers; some said that it did not exist and never had done, and that the name and stories about it had just been invented. In undertaking its conquest Caesar was extending the Roman Empire beyond the limits of the inhabited world. (3) He made two crossings to the island from the coast of Gaul opposite and worsted the enemy in a number of battles without gaining much advantage for his own men (there was nothing really worth taking from men who led such wretchedly poor lives). So the war ended rather contrary to his hopes, but he did exact hostages from the king and impose tribute before he left the island.

A similar assessment is made by Dio.

230.

DIO 39.53 (2) What had previously been unknown was now revealed; what had been unheard of was now accessible. So they treated their hopes for the outcome of these achievements as already realized and prided themselves on all that they expected to obtain as if it was in their hands already. For this reason they voted to celebrate twenty days of thanksgiving.

Suetonius (*Div. Jul.* 25.2) also says that nothing was known about the Britons before.

Some other opinions:

231.
VELLEIUS 2.46 (1) Not content with his good fortune in winning numerous victories, and killing and capturing countless thousand enemies, he took his army across to Britain, in quest, you might say, of another world to add to the Roman Empire which he had already enlarged.

232.
STRABO 4.5 (3) The late Caesar twice crossed over to the island; however he was quick to return, without having achieved anything much or penetrated far inland ... However he won two or three victories over the Britons, even though he had only taken two legions of his army across with him; and he brought back hostages and slaves and plenty of other plunder.

> The contemporary evidence of Cicero about the second expedition to Britain (see nos. **256** ff.) makes it seem that the country was not so rich in spoils as Strabo says.

233.
TACITUS *Agr.* 13 (2) The deified Julius was the first Roman to invade Britain with an army. His campaign was successful in that it frightened the inhabitants and gave him command of the coast; but he could be said to have shown the way to his successors rather than handed them an actual possession.

Compare these different evaluations of Caesar's achievement in Britain on his first expedition. Would it be true to say that the fact of his landing there was of more importance than the material success he enjoyed? Would Caesar have been satisfied with the results of his mission?

In spite of the public tribute, some dislike of Caesar was evident even in non-political circles:

234.
SUETONIUS *Div. Jul.* 73. Caesar made no secret of the fact that Valerius Catullus had blackened his name irrevocably by his verses about Mamurra; but when Catullus apologized, Caesar

invited him to dinner the same day and remained as friendly with his father as he had always been.

Mamurra was a knight with a high post on Caesar's staff in Gaul (Pliny *N.H.* 36.48). The wealth he derived from serving Caesar was notorious (Cic. *ad Att.* 7.7.6, written in 49) and he is reputed to have been the first man in Rome to put a marble facing on the walls of his house.

235.

CATULLUS 29.

Who can bear the sight, who can put up with it, / except for one sunk in debauchery, gluttony and gambling, / that Mamurra should have for himself what Further Gaul / and distant Britain once owned? /

(5) Romulus, you little sod, can you put up with the sight? /
But you are sunk in debauchery, gluttony and gambling . . . /

(21) . . . Why do you support this good-for-nothing? What can he do / except gobble up succulent legacies? /
Was it really for him that you, †the most powerful men in Rome†, / son and father-in-law, have ruined everything?

The date of this poem is usually fixed in the winter of 55/4 by the reference to Britain and the marriage tie between Caesar and Pompey which was broken by Julia's death in August 54 (see nos. **251** ff.). 'Romulus' refers to Caesar, and hints at a possible ambition of Caesar to become king and second founder of Rome. The names of Caesar and Mamurra are linked even less ambiguously and less decorously in Catullus 57.

VI. The Ascendancy of Pompey

The partnership was now effectively reduced to two, as Crassus was away in the East and would never return. Pompey, as the man on the scene, held the initiative, whereas Caesar could only rely on indirect influence. Although they combined their powers sufficiently to neutralize a potentially hostile consul, there were already signs of strain in the relationship. There was for instance some disagreement between them about whom to promote for the consulship. In the end Caesar's candidate was discredited when an unsavour conspiracy came to light, apparently at Pompey's instigation. A more serious breach occurred in the autumn when Pompey's wife, Julia, died, with the child who might have brought father and grandfather closer together. Caesar could do little to counteract Pompey's growing influence apart from securing the wholesale co-operation of Cicero. In Gaul his fortunes were low, and he could not even make his usual journey to Italy in the winter.

So circumstances conspired to give Pompey a position of dominance at Rome, which was further enhanced by news of the death of Crassus in 53. And yet Pompey made no move to exploit the advantage he had obtained. What then was the extent of his ambition?

A. Pompey's position at Rome in 54

THE ELECTIONS

Pompey, by virtue of the provincial command which he now held (see nos. **195** ff.) was not allowed into the city of Rome. However he stayed well within reach (ostensibly to look after the grain-supply) and left the governing of Spain to his officers. This may have had a stultifying effect on all political activity, but it was not a situation in which much positive influence could be exercised. That could only be re-established by finding more compliant magistrates for the following year.

236.

CICERO *ad Q.f.* 2.13 (15a) [Rome, June 54] (5) This is how things are at Rome. There is some hope of the elections being held, but no guarantee. There is also a suspicion that we shall have a dictatorship, but one can't be sure about that either. There is no activity in the forum, but that is a sign that the state is dying, not acquiescing. The opinions I express in the Senate are such that other people endorse them more than I do myself.

The four main candidates in the consular elections were: C. Memmius, who had once been an opponent of Caesar (see nos. **48, 49**), but was now apparently reconciled; Cn. Domitius Calvinus, later one of Caesar's generals in the civil war (see also no. **174**); M. Aemilius Scaurus, famous for the lavish games he put on as aedile in 58; and M. Valerius Messalla.

237.

CICERO *ad Att.* 4.15 [Rome, 27 July 54] (7) Now follow me to the Campus. Bribery is rampant . . . Memmius has the backing of all Caesar's resources. Between him and Domitius the consuls have arranged a pact, the nature of which I daren't entrust to a letter. Pompey is loud in protest; he is supporting Scaurus, but whether that is in earnest or just a front nobody knows. No one has got a nose in front; the qualities of them all are levelled by money. Messalla is lagging behind; he isn't short of ambition or friends, but the consular coalition and Pompey are against him. If you ask me, the elections are likely to be postponed.

238.

CICERO *ad Att.* 4.16 [Rome, July 54] (6) I don't quite know how to answer your question about Messalla; I've never seen such evenly matched candidates. You know what support he has. Scaurus has had an action brought against him by Triarius, but, you know, this has not won much sympathy for him. Still his aedileship left no unpleasant memories, and the reputation left by his father will count for something with the country voters. The two plebeian candidates have little to choose between them: Domitius has powerful friends and his popular shows will help him considerably; Memmius is well in with Caesar's soldiers and leans heavily on Pompey's Gaul. If that isn't enough to get him in, it is thought that someone will stop the elections taking place until Caesar arrives.

'Pompey's Gaul' was the area round Picenum where his family had property. Does this then mean that Memmius had the backing of Pompey as well as Caesar, in spite of what is said in no. **237**? If so, what would he stand to gain by revealing the plot (see no. **239**), and why should Pompey have encouraged him to do so?

239.
CICERO *ad Att.* 4.17 [Rome, 1 Oct. 54] (2) Memmius has put a torch to the consuls' disgraceful behaviour by reading out in the Senate the agreement they had made with him and his fellow-candidate, Domitius; by this the consuls were each to receive 400,000 sesterces from both of them, if elected to the consulships ... The agreement was not just a verbal one apparently, but properly drawn up and documented, with money-orders from the bankers and the sums entered into the appropriate accounts. Whereupon Memmius revealed the whole thing with all the evidence, at the prompting of Pompey. Appius was not at all put out: of course he had nothing to lose. To his colleague it was a severe blow, from which he hasn't really recovered. (3) For breaking up the ring against Calvinus' wishes, Memmius has dropped out altogether, and his fate is sealed all the more because we now learn that his disclosure was considerably resented by Caesar. Our friend Messalla and his fellow-competitor Domitius have been very liberal with the people and could not be more popular. They must be certainties for the consulship.

240.
CICERO *ad Q.f.* 3.8 [Rome, late Nov. 54] (3) In reckoning Messalla and Domitius as certainties for the consulship, you follow my opinion exactly. I'll answer to Caesar for Messalla's attitude. Memmius pins his hopes on Caesar's arrival; surely that is misguided. At any rate he is out in the cold at the moment — and Scaurus has long since been thrown over by Pompey. (4) Things are still undecided; and the postponement of the elections looks as if it will lead to an interregnum. The *optimates* are not pleased by the rumours of dictatorship, and I am even less so by the current gossip. But people are afraid to do anything, and the whole situation is at a standstill. Pompey has said in public that he doesn't want it; to me earlier he made no such disavowal.

In the event the elections were postponed till half-way through the following year (see nos. **271** ff.). Cicero himself was disenchanted with politics in spite of attempts made to involve him more closely (see nos. **263** ff.), and limited his activity to helping Milo in his bid to be elected consul the following year (Cic. *ad Q.f.* 3.8.6, 3.9.2).

241.

CICERO *ad Q.f.* 3.9 [Rome, Dec. 54] (3) By the way — there still hasn't been anything done about a dictator after all. Pompey is away; Appius is agitating; Hirrus is plotting; there are plenty of people ready to veto; the populace are unconcerned; the leaders are not in favour. I'm keeping quiet.

> For Appius Claudius, see no. **242** n.; for C. Lucilius Hirrus, see no. **273.**

THE LAW COURTS

In spite of Cicero's disenchantment with politics, his forensic activity was unabated, and at least eight major speeches can be attributed to him during the year 54. The most important of these were undertaken at the request of Caesar or Pompey, and Cicero's compliance, even for such uncongenial clients as Vatinius and Gabinius, shows the extent of his capitulation.

242.

CICERO *ad Att.* 4.15 [Rome, 27 July 54] (9) I have undertaken the defence of Messius, who had been given a post on Caesar's staff by Appius but was recalled by Servilius to stand trial in person . . . Then I am preparing for the case of Drusus and after that Scaurus. These are fine names to put at the head of my speeches. Perhaps they will even be joined by those of the consuls designate — and if Scaurus isn't included among that lot, he may well be in trouble at his trial.

> Messius was the tribune of 57 who had agitated for Cicero's recall and had also proposed wide powers for Pompey (see no. **155**). Appius Claudius was a consul of the year, and Servilius Isauricus a praetor. For Scaurus, see no. **237.**

243.

CICERO *ad Q.f.* 2.15 (16) [Rome, Aug. 54] (3) On the day I write, Drusus has been acquitted on a charge of fraudulent collusion thanks to the *tribuni aerarii;* there were only four votes in it, and the Senate and Knights had both voted against him. This same afternoon I am going to defend Vatinius, which should be quite simple. The elections have been postponed until September. Scaurus' case comes up any day now; I shall not fail him.

> *Tribuni aerarii* (= Treasury Tribunes): a class of wealthy citizens who, as a result of reforms made by Pompey when he was consul in 70, now provided one-third of the jury panel. Cicero's reasons for defending Vatinius were later set out in the long letter to Lentulus Spinther (*ad Fam.* 1.9); see no. **206.**

The most notorious trial was that of Aulus Gabinius who had abandoned his province of Syria to help reinstate Ptolemy in Egypt (cf. nos. **164–8**). The tax-collectors complained that in his absence they had suffered from the depredations of piracy (Dio 39.59.1).

244.

DIO 39.55 (1) It was at about this time that Ptolemy was restored to the throne of his kingdom, even though the Romans had voted against helping him and were still highly indignant at the amount of bribery he had perpetrated. (2) The restoration was the work of Pompey and Gabinius; the weight of power and money counted for so much more than the decree of the Senate and People (3) that when Gabinius, then governor of Syria, received instructions from Pompey and undertook the campaign, they restored the king without paying any attention to the oracles of the Sibyl or the wishes of the state. Pompey's motives were charitable, but Gabinius' pecuniary.

Gabinius was first tried for treason (*maiestas*), and Cicero's initial reaction was delight at the discomfiture of this creature of Pompey's, who as consul in 58 had done nothing to restrain the rampant Clodius (cf. no. **52**).

245.

CICERO *ad Q.f.* 3.1 [Rome, Sept. 54] (15) Gabinius is still being prosecuted by three parties: by Lucius Lentulus, son of the priest, who has now brought a charge of treason; by Tiberius Nero, who has the backing of the *optimates;* and by the tribune Gaius Memmius [not the same Memmius as in nos. **237–40**] together with Lucius [Ateius] Capito. Gabinius reached Rome on Sept. 19th, looking quite frightful and thoroughly disreputable. But I wouldn't dare bet on anything with these law-courts. Because of Cato's indisposition, the charge for extortion has not yet been brought. Pompey is trying very hard to win my favour again; as yet he has got nowhere and, so long as I retain a vestige of independence, he never will. [The letter was delayed for some days, and there are various later additions:]

(24) What else? Oh yes. Gabinius entered the city on the night of Sept. 27th; and today at 2 o'clock, when he was due to face the treason charge according to the edict of Alfius, he was nearly crushed by a huge crowd all demonstrating their hatred. He really is the end.

246.

CICERO *ad Q.f.* 3.2 [Rome, 11 Oct. 54] (1) Gabinius really is pushed — but of course our friend Pompey may upset the whole shooting-match, in defiance of God and man.

See also Cic. *ad Att.* 4.18.3, written at about the same time.

Cicero himself gave evidence for the prosecution, though he did not actually lead the attack.

247.

DIO 39.62 (2) Gabinius was tried on the most serious charge first, that of restoring Ptolemy. Just about the whole populace surged into the court and showed great readiness to tear him apart, especially as Pompey was away and Cicero's attack was particularly ruthless. But he was acquitted in spite of the general feeling; (3) for not only had he disbursed enormous sums of money, proportionate to the gravity of the charge, but he also had vigorous support from the friends of Pompey and Caesar; they maintained that the Sibyl referred to a quite different situation and a different king; and, most important of all, the verses made no mention of a punishment for doing as he had.

248.

CICERO *ad Q.f.* 3.4 [Rome, 24 Oct. 54] (1) Gabinius has been acquitted. Nothing could have been more infantile than the

E

performance put up by the accuser Lentulus and his supporters, nothing more despicable that the behaviour of the jury. But even Lentulus would have had the better of him if it hadn't been for the remarkable vigour and appeals of Pompey and the ominous rumours of dictatorship. As it was, even with an accuser and a jury like that, 32 of the 70 votes recorded were in favour of condemning him.

Immediately after his acquittal, he was recalled to face trial on the lesser charge of extortion (Dio 39.55.5); and this time Cicero was persuaded to undertake his defence.

249.

DIO 39.63 (3) Pompey had been away looking after the corn-supply and trying to make good the destruction caused by the flooding of the Tiber, but he was still in Italy and hurried back to be in time for the first trial. In fact he was too late [cf. no. **248** however], but this time did not leave the city precincts until the second trial was over. (4) As his proconsular office prevented him from entering the city, the people collected outside the *pomerium*; there he made a long speech in defence of Gabinius and read out a letter Caesar had sent him supporting the man. (5) He made an appeal to the jurors and even persuaded Cicero to withdraw from the prosecution and take up the defence of Gabinius instead (this made people call Cicero a deserter more than ever). But even this did not do Gabinius any good; he was convicted and exiled.

250.

CICERO *Rab. Post.* 32. My reason, Gaius Memmius, for defending Gabinius was that we had become friends again. I am not sorry that my hostility is temporary, while my friendship is everlasting. (33) If you think that I defended him just to avoid giving offence to Pompey, then you have gone badly wrong in your estimation of both him and me. Pompey would never have wanted me to do anything against my will just for his sake, and I, who have always valued most highly the freedom of all my fellow-citizens, would never have discarded my own.

How convincing is this piece of self-justification? Bear in mind Cicero's tendency to try and back both sides at once, as in nos. **165** and **267**.

How should we judge the political significance of these trials? Most of the people brought into court enjoyed the patronage of Caesar or Pompey or both, and, so far as we can tell, this was usually enough to get them acquitted; but the ultimate conviction of Gabinius must be reckoned as something of a victory for the *optimates*.

THE DEATH OF JULIA

Later writers generally agree that the most unfortunate single blow struck at the partnership (and hence at the stability of the country) was the death of Julia to whom Pompey had been quite devoted. Without her, the link between Pompey and Caesar was reduced to a matter of political expediency.

251.

PLUTARCH *Caes.* 23 (4) [When Caesar returned from Britain to Gaul in 54,] ... he found letters from his friends in Rome which were just about to be sent across to him; they told him of the death of his daughter — she died in childbirth at Pompey's house. Both Pompey and Caesar were very distressed; but their friends were also alarmed at the dissolution of the relationship which had alone guaranteed peace and harmony in the ailing state. To make matters worse, the child died immediately afterwards, having only survived its mother by a few days.

> According to Seneca 6.14.3 (from the dialogue 'On Consolation'), Caesar was still in Britain when he heard the news. See also Val. Max. 4.6.4.

252.

CICERO *ad Q.f.* 3.1 [Rome, Sept. 54] (17) Just as I was folding this letter up on Sept. 20th, the post arrived from you and Caesar, having been 26 days in coming. I *was* distressed, and *how* sorry I felt, reading Caesar's charming letter; but the more charming it was, the greater the distress I felt at his tragedy.

253.

DIO 39.64. At this time Pompey's wife died in giving birth to a daughter. And for some reason or other — perhaps a concerted move by the friends of Caesar and Pompey, or by people who wanted to ingratiate themselves — her body was snatched up as soon as the eulogy in the forum was completed, and buried in the Campus Martius, in spite of all Domitius' attempts to prevent it; amongst other things, he claimed that it was sacrilege to bury her in a sacred place without a special decree.

> According to Livy *Per.* 106, Vell. 2.47.2, Suet. *Div. Jul.* 26.1, Julia's child was a son, not a daughter.
> For Pompey's subsequent remarriage, see nos. **314** f.

B. *Caesar and Cicero*

THE SECOND INVASION OF BRITAIN

Caesar must have thought the political situation safe enough for him to venture to Britain again. Although he himself is silent about what his objectives were, the size and nature of the expedition has led most later writers to agree that he was intending to conquer the whole island.

254.

DIO 40.1 (2) When the weather allowed him, he sailed over to Britain again; his excuse was that they had failed to send all the hostages they had promised, thinking that he would not trouble them again having once returned empty-handed; but the truth of the matter was that he had an obsessive desire for the island and, if that pretext had not presented itself, he would have had no difficulty in finding another.

Caesar had begun preparations for a full-scale expedition as soon as he had returned to Gaul in the winter of 55. He ordered large numbers of new ships carefully made to specifications designed to overcome the major difficulties he had met on his first expedition (*B.G.* 5.1.1–2). He also refused to get involved in wars with either the Pirustae or the Treveri and settled both of their disturbances by diplomacy (*B.G.* 5.1.9, 5.4.1). The expedition was delayed by contrary winds for a month (*B.G.* 5.7.3), but sailed in early July with five legions and two thousand cavalry (*B.G.* 5.8.2). Although he succeeded in crossing the Thames (*B.G.* 5.18) and capturing one of the strongholds of the Kentish king Cassivelaunus (*B.G.* 5.21), he must have been disappointed with his overall achievement. In spite of his precautions, forty of his ships again suffered from storm-damage (*B.G.* 5.10.2) and his armoured troops were at a constant disadvantage in face of the Britons' mobile guerilla tactics. Only when the Britons tried a combined attack on the Roman camp were they decisively defeated (*B.G.* 5.22.1–2).

255.

CAESAR *B.G.* 5.22 (3) The news of this battle, taken with the number of losses sustained, the devastation of his territories, and above all the defection of other states, so alarmed Cassivelaunus that he opened negotiations about surrendering to Caesar by way of Commius. (4) Caesar had already decided to winter on the continent for fear of a sudden outbreak of rebellion; anyway there was not much of the summer left, and the Britons would easily be able to hold out that long. So he demanded hostages and fixed the amount of tribute that Britain should pay yearly to the Roman people.

> The reason which Caesar gives for deciding not to spend the winter in Britain (even though he was equipped to do so) is not fully convincing: if he was genuinely afraid of a new Gallic uprising, it is strange that he was not more alert and less alarmed when the rebellion *did* break out (*B.G.* 5.28.1); and stranger still that Caesar should have left his army, without even his lieutenants knowing where he was (*B.G.* 5.29.2). The Latin would as easily mean 'because of a sudden uprising in Gaul' — but his army had been in winter-quarters for two weeks before the trouble started; and then it came as a surprise.

Cicero had private sources of information from Gaul and Britain: his brother Quintus who had been on Caesar's staff since at any rate February 54 (Cic. *ad Q.f.* 2.10(12).4–5); and Gaius Trebatius Testa whom Cicero had recommended to Caesar a month or two earlier (Cic. *ad Fam.* 7.5.1). The disappointing nature of their reports can be seen from Cicero's reaction.

256.

CICERO *ad Fam.* 7.7 [Rome, May 54, to Trebatius] (1) I hear that in Britain there is no gold and no silver. If that is so, I suggest that you find a war-chariot to capture and hurry back to join me as soon as you can.

257.

CICERO *ad Q.f.* 3.1 [Arpinum/Rome, Sept. 54] (10) On the situation in Britain I understand from your letter that there is no cause for alarm, and none for rejoicing either . . . (25) Caesar sent me a letter from Britain on Sept. 1st; it reached me on the 27th, containing some reasonably satisfactory news about things over there.

258.

CICERO *ad Att.* 4.17 [Rome, 1 Oct. 54] (6) There is some specu-
lation about the outcome of the British campaign. Reports agree
that the approaches to the islands are guarded by remarkable
cliffs. And it has also been discovered that there isn't a scrap of
silver anywhere in the island, and the only kind of war-spoil we
can hope for is slaves; but I don't suppose you'll find any among
them with a literary or musical education.

259.

CICERO *ad Att.* 4.18 [Rome, Oct. 54] (5) On October 24th I
received letters from Caesar and my brother Quintus, sent off
from the nearest part of the coast of Britain on Sept. 25th. Britain
has been dealt with and hostages have been received; there was no
plunder, but tribute has been demanded; now they are bringing
the army back.

Estimates of Caesar's achievement vary, depending on whether it is
regarded as a military or a political venture. See nos. **230** ff.

260.

FLORUS 1.45 (19) Caesar was satisfied with what he had done —
he was after all only out to acquire a reputation, not a province —
and returned with more spoils than before. The very Ocean
favoured him with greater calm, as if to admit that it had met its
match.

Is Florus right, or should we regard the second expedition as a failure?

CAESAR'S POSITION AT ROME

For the maintenance of his influence at Rome Caesar had to rely on the
work of his agents, such as Balbus and Oppius, and friendly politicians.
He was particularly anxious to have the goodwill of Cicero, whose support
would lend his name a greater air of respectability, and perhaps make him
more acceptable to the conservative ranks of the Senate. Cicero accepted
the bait whole-heartedly — with his brother Quintus on Caesar's staff, it
would have been impolitic to do otherwise. For a time potential opposition
to Caesar was stifled.

261.

CICERO *ad Q.f.* 2.13 (15a) [Rome, June 54] (3) I asked Caesar to get Marcus Curtius a post as military tribune (Domitius would have thought I was pulling his leg if I had asked him; his daily joke is saying that he hasn't even got enough power to make a military tribune).

262.

SUETONIUS *Nero* 2 (2) When Domitius was consul he tried to have Caesar recalled from commanding the armies in Gaul and himself named as his successor by the rival faction.

Even if this is true, the attempt was totally unsuccessful.

263.

CICERO *ad Q.f.* 2.11 (13) [Rome, June 54] (1) As you know, I have long been singing the praises of your Caesar. Believe me, he is my bosom friend, and I'm making no attempt to break the bond.

See also Cic. *ad Q.f.* 2.10(12).5.

264.

CICERO *ad Q.f.* 2.13 (15a) [Rome, June 54] (1) I received your letter from Placentia on the 2nd, the day I arrived in Rome; the next day another from Bladeno, together with Caesar's kind, attentive and charming letter. His attitude is important, very important, as it helps greatly for winning distinction and the highest respect.

Whether Caesar expected from Cicero any other services apart from the defence of his clients at Rome (cf. nos. **242** ff.), is open to question. The language of no. **266** suggests that Caesar may even have wanted him to stand as consul (it would be just ten years since his last consulship), when on his return from Britain he learnt of Memmius' disclosure (see no. **239**); perhaps it was just this sort of thing that Pompey wished to forestall by engaging Cicero's services himself.

265.

CICERO *ad Q.f.* 3.1 [Rome, Sept. 54] (18) You say in the middle of your letter that I am going to become one of Pompey's staff on

Sept. 13th; but I've heard nothing about it. Anyway I wrote to tell Caesar that Pompey had not got his message either from Oppius or Vibullius about my staying in Rome.

> Oppius, as appears from other parts of this letter, was one of Caesar's agents in Rome; Vibullius was probably one of Pompey's.

266.

CICERO *ad Q.f.* 3.6 [Tusculum, late Oct. 54] (3) I am absolutely delighted by all that you write about Caesar's affection for me; I am not depending overmuch on the offers he holds out: I do not thirst for public offices and I do not yearn for glory. I prefer looking forward to the continuance of his goodwill rather than the fulfilment of his promises.

> Cicero, true to his principles (cf. nos. **165, 242** ff.), did his best to accommodate both Caesar and Pompey.

267.

CICERO *ad Att.* 4.19 [Rome, Nov. 54] (2) Quintus tells me that he was offered a complete choice of winter-quarters by Caesar. One can't help loving that man more than any of the others. Oh, but had I told you? I've been appointed to Pompey's staff, so I won't be in Rome after Jan. 13th. It seems to fit in with things rather nicely.

> Cicero does not in fact seem to have undertaken this mission.

268.

CICERO *ad Fam.* 1.9 [Rome, Dec. 54, to Lentulus Spinther] (21) My brother Quintus is on Caesar's staff and anything, however small, that I have done, or even said, on Caesar's behalf has been welcomed with such thanks as to make me feel that Caesar is under some obligation to me. This has enabled me to use as my own his unequalled influence and enormous resources.

> A substantial part of these 'enormous resources' was spent on bringing Caesar's name to the public notice again by financing some massive public buildings.

269.

CICERO *ad Att.* 4.17 [Rome, 1 Oct. 54] (7) We friends of Caesar, Oppius and I, that is — don't explode ! — have thought nothing of spending sixty million sesterces on the work you used to speak so highly of, enlarging the Forum and extending it as far as the Hall of Liberty. We couldn't do a bargain with the private owners for anything less. But still, it will be quite magnificent in the end. On the Campus Martius we are going to make a marble voting-enclosure for the tribal assembly; it will have a roof and a marble colonnade all the way round, a mile long.

270.

PLINY *N.H.* 36 (103) Julius Caesar paid 100,000,000 sesterces just for the land on which his Forum was built.

C. A year of inactivity (53)

THE CONSULAR ELECTIONS

The year started with the offices of state again unfilled, and all eyes were turned on Pompey. One alternative much canvassed was that he should be appointed dictator, and it was not until half-way through the year that hostile pressure or his own disinclination finally persuaded him to reject the idea.

271.

DIO 40.45 (1) During these same years there were many distur-bances in the city, particularly over the elections; as a result it was only after six months that [Cn. Domitius] Calvinus and [M. Valerius] Messalla were elected consuls ... (3) sometimes it was the omens which prevented the elections taking place by refusing to favour the *interreges*. But it was the tribunes who did most to prevent the remaining offices being filled, by exercising such control over the affairs of the city that they even took over the praetors' jobs ... (4) The tribunes all put up a number of ob-structive suggestions, such as that 'chiliarchs' should be elected instead of consuls, so that there would be more magistrates, as had once been the case. (5) When no one listened to them, they declared that at least Pompey ought to be made dictator. Using this pretext, they secured the longest possible delay, as Pompey himself was away and the people in the city would not undertake to vote for it — the memory of Sulla's cruelty made them all hate the institution; on the other hand, such was their fear of Pompey that they did not want to refuse to elect him either. 46 (1) At long last he appeared in person; he had the grace to refuse the dictatorship offered him and made arrangements for the election of the consuls.

> Chiliarch: originally a military officer; the term means 'captain of a thousand'.

272.

APPIAN *B.C.* 2.19 (70) The yearly consuls despaired of leading an army or going on campaign, as they were debarred by the power of the Three. The more degraded of them looked to the public treasury and the election of their successors to supply them with the profit they were unable to get from campaigning. (71) This made the 'good' men shy away from holding office altogether, and once the city went eight months without magistrates as a result of this disorder. Pompey purposely took no action, so as to create the need for a dictator. 20 (72) This became common talk — that the only remedy for the present troubles was for one man to take control; the man they chose had to be powerful, but not oppressive (this pointed to Pompey); a man who commanded a large enough army and gave the appearance of being friendly with the people besides having the status necessary to lead the Senate; he must be temperate in his habits and self-controlled, while at any rate giving the illusion of being affable and approachable. (73) In public Pompey discounted the likelihood of being made dictator, but under cover he was in fact doing all he could to encourage it and purposely did nothing about the disorderliness of the state and the anarchy which resulted from it.

273.

PLUTARCH *Pomp.* 54 (2) When Pompey saw that the disposal of the magistracies was not going in accordance with his wishes because of the bribery practised by the citizens, he allowed the state offices to go unfilled. This at once gave rise to a widespread

rumour about a dictatorship; it was first brought out into the open
by the tribune Lucilius, who boldly recommended the people to
elect Pompey dictator. But when Cato attacked him, he was nearly
expelled from his tribunate. In Pompey's defence many of his
friends came forward, saying that he had no need of the office and
no desire for it either. (3) This drew Cato's support for Pompey
and an exhortation to concern himself with restoring public order;
Pompey was, for a time, shamed into doing so, and Domitius and
Messalla were made consuls.

> Compare this account with the two preceding; do they between them
> give a plausible and consistent explanation of why Pompey did not
> accept the dictatorship?

274.

DIO 40.46 (2) The consuls passed a resolution that no praetor or
consul should obtain a command abroad until five years had
elapsed since the time they left office; their intention was to curtail
the scramble for power by not letting them go straight from their
magistracy to a position of influence.

> This seems to have been the only significant legislation passed during
> the year (cf. no. 319). Most of the energy of the consuls was taken up in
> controlling the violence of the magisterial candidates for the following
> year. Even so the year ended with the elections still not held.

Cicero's correspondence is limited this year: the series of letters to his
brother stops and there are none to Atticus. In the dozen or so that can
be assigned to this period there is little mention of political activity.

275.

CICERO ad Fam. 2.3 [Rome, 53, to C. Scribonius Curio, quaestor
in Asia] (1) To put it briefly, the situation is such that, believe me,
when you return you will find it easier to win the highest offices in
the state by virtue of your natural qualities, application, and good
fortune, than by putting on public displays; to be able to provide
such spectacles is a sign of affluence, not good character, and
excites no admiration. In fact everyone is sick and tired of them.

276.

CICERO ad Fam. 2.4 [Rome, 53, to C. Scribonius Curio] (1) Am I
to fill my letters with jokes? Heavens, I don't think there's a single

citizen who can bring himself to laugh nowadays. Or should I write something more serious? What serious subject could Cicero write to Curio about except politics? But then such is my position here that I haven't the courage to write what I feel, nor the inclination to write what I don't.

Only the forthcoming elections seem to have aroused Cicero's interest, because of his patronage of Milo (cf. nos. **290** ff.).

277.

CICERO *ad Fam.* 2.6 [Rome, July 53, to C. Scribonius Curio] (3) I have focused my whole attention on getting Milo elected consul; to this end I have concentrated all my efforts and energies, all my powers of thought and application, in fact the whole of my mental resources ... We have got all this in our favour: the support of the *optimates*, won, as I hope you realize, by his defence of my case in his tribunate; the support of the people, because of his lavish public shows and natural generosity; the backing of the younger generation and the people who control votes, because of his great popularity — or perhaps assiduity — in that field; and then my own electoral influence, which may not be as powerful, but is at least well-tried, honest, and under obligation to him; this may perhaps even give it additional influence.

THE DEATH OF CRASSUS

Some time that autumn must have come the news that Crassus had been destroyed with his army at the battle of Carrhae (for full details, see Plut. *Crass.* 18–33, Dio 40.17–27). The political repercussions could not but be considerable: the partnership was now reduced to two, and the Knights no longer had a champion in Rome.

278.

OVID *Fasti* 6. (Under *ad. V. Id. Jun.*, the Feast of Vesta: June 9th.) (397) Crassus on the Euphrates lost his eagles, his son, and his men, and finally his own life.

279.

DIO 40.27 (2) Crassus was among the fallen, either killed by one of his own men to prevent his being captured alive, or by the enemy when he had been severely wounded. (3) Anyway that was the end of him; and there is a tradition which says that the Parthians in mockery poured molten gold into his mouth. For in spite of his great wealth, he was so obsessed by money that he pitied as poor anyone unable to support an enrolled legion out of his own pocket.

REVOLTS IN GAUL

If Caesar had any thoughts of direct intervention to counteract Pompey's growing importance, these were frustrated by a series of insurrections in Gaul.

280.

CAESAR *B.G.* 5.24 (1) Drought had made that year's harvest in Gaul a poor one, and Caesar was therefore compelled to change his usual wintering policy by allocating his legions to a number of different states [these states were: the Morini, the Nervii, the Remi, the Esubii, the Bellovaci (?), and the Eburones] ... (6) This dispersion of the legions was thought by Caesar to be the best way of meeting the grain shortage — (7) although in fact none of the legions were quartered more than a hundred miles apart, except for the one under Lucius Roscius which had been assigned to the quietest and most placid part of Gaul [the Esubii]. (8) Caesar himself decided to stay in Gaul until he heard that all the legions had reached their destinations and fortified their quarters.

> Had Caesar really decided to stay in Gaul, in spite of the situation at Rome? In *B.G.* 5.29.2 Sabinus is made to say 'I think Caesar must have set out for Italy; ... the Eburones wouldn't otherwise have approached our camp with such contempt, if he were still in the country.'

A fortnight after winter-quarters had been established, the Eburones came out in revolt. Their leader Ambiorix lured the nearest Roman garrison out of its camp with the offer of a safe-conduct and then destroyed it in an ambush (*B.G.* 5.26–37). He also persuaded the Nervii to attack the garrison under Quintus Cicero, but Cicero managed to hang on until Caesar arrived and drove the Gauls off (*B.G.* 5.38–52).

281.

CAESAR *B.G.* 5.53 (2) When news of Caesar's victory reached the ears of the Treveri, Indutiomarus, who had decided to attack

Labienus' camp [in Remi territory] on the following day, withdrew in the night and led his troops back into their own territory. (3) Caesar then sent Fabius and his legion back to their quarters [among the Morini]; he then decided that three legions should spend the winter in separate camps around Samarobriva [Amiens] and determined to stay with the army himself all the time as there was so much unrest in Gaul.

The Gauls kept up their intrigues throughout the winter, but the most serious threat, from the Treveri, was quelled when Labienus defeated them and killed Indutiomarus (*B.G.* 5.54–58).

282.

CAESAR *B.G.* 6.1 (1) As Caesar had many reasons for supposing that there would be an even greater disturbance in Gaul, he decided to use his officers, Marcus Silanus, Gaius Antistius Reginus, and Titus Sextius, to recruit some new troops. (2) At the same time he sent a request to Pompey, who in spite of his pro-consular command still remained near Rome in the public interest, asking him to mobilize and send on to him the troops from Cisalpine Gaul who had sworn the oath of allegiance to him when he was consul. (3) He thought it would have a considerable psychological effect on Gaul in the future if they saw that the resources of man-power in Italy were enough not just to patch up any immediate war-losses but even to increase the total number of forces. (4) Pompey complied in deference to the demands of public interest and private friendship, and the recruiting by Caesar's officers was speedily carried out. So before the end of the winter, three legions had been formed and brought up, thus making double the number of legions lost [to the Eburones].

The campaigns of the following year were mainly concerned to stamp out incipient revolt, or forestall the threat of it. His chief target was the Treveri tribe which, undeterred by the death of Indutiomarus had been sending frequent requests for help to the Germans.

283.

CAESAR *B.G.* 6.2 (3) So Caesar thought that he had better make his campaigning plans earlier than usual. 3 (1) Accordingly, before winter was even over, he made a surprise march into the territory of the Nervii with the four nearest legions; (2) before they had time to collect their forces or run away, Caesar had captured a large number of prisoners and cattle (which he gave to the soldiers as war-spoils), and compelled them to surrender and give hostages. (3) After this speedy despatch of the matter, he led his troops back into winter-quarters.

He then called a Gallic conference at Lutetia (Paris). As the Senones and Carnutes stayed away, he marched against them, and they rapidly came to terms (*B.G.* 6.3.4–4.5). He next sent a punitive expedition against the Menapii, potential allies of the Treveri, and compelled them to sue for peace (*B.G.* 6.5–6). The Treveri themselves attacked Labienus, but were lured into a bad position by the feigned flight of the Romans and again defeated (*B.G.* 6.7–8).

284.

CAESAR *B.G.* 6.9 (1) Caesar himself, who had travelled from the Menapii to the Treveri, now decided to cross the Rhine. His reasons were: (2) first, that the Treveri had received help against him from there; second, that he wanted to prevent Ambiorix taking refuge among them. . . . [The Ubii at once sent representatives to affirm their loyalty] . . . (8) Caesar looked into the case and discovered that the assistance had been sent by the Suebi; so he accepted what the Ubii said and made detailed inquiries about the ways of access to the territory of the Suebi.

[He learned that the Suebi had retired to the most distant part of their country and decided that it would be dangerous to pursue them; so he returned to Gaul, first destroying the German end of the bridge over the Rhine (*B.G.* 6.9–10, 29). Chapters 11–28 of Book 6 are taken up with a description of Gallic and German customs.]

Caesar then went after Ambiorix 'when the crops were beginning to ripen' (*B.G.* 6.29.4). He, unwilling to risk open battle, did not assemble an army, but told everyone to take independent action (*B.G.* 6.31.2). Caesar therefore established a base at Aduatuca and divided his army into three.

285.

CAESAR *B.G.* 6.33 (1) He ordered Titus Labienus to take three legions in the direction of the coast to the land bordering on the Menapii; (2) he sent Gaius Trebonius with the same number of troops to ravage the territory next to the Aduatuci; (3) he himself decided to go with the other three legions to the river Scheldt, which flows into the Meuse, at the far end of the Ardennes, as he heard that Ambiorix had made for that area with a few cavalry. (4) On his departure he assured them that he would be back within a week, knowing that a further distribution of food would then be due to the legion left at the base-camp. (5) He encouraged Labienus and Trebonius to return by the same date if they could conveniently do so, so that they could discuss further policy and make a new start in the war, in the light of the information they had acquired about the enemy.

As the Eburones used guerilla tactics, Caesar decided that it would be dangerous and expensive to mount an all-out campaign against them.

286.

CAESAR *B.G.* 6.34 (8) So he sent messengers round the neighbouring states, encouraging them with the prospects of spoil to join in looting the Eburones. He preferred to jeopardize the life of Gauls in the forests, rather than his own legionaries, and hoped that in retribution for its criminal action the tribe would be obliterated, name and all, by the massive incursions from all sides.

The Sugambri were among the German tribes who heard this general invitation to plunder. They therefore sent 2,000 cavalry across the Rhine and helped themselves to the Eburones' cattle; but they were then tempted by the prospect of richer spoils to attack the small Roman garrison left at Aduatuca. The Romans, commanded by Quintus Cicero, were taken by surprise, with five cohorts out in the fields collecting food. However all except one detachment managed to get safely back into the beleaguered camp, and the Germans withdrew as soon as it was fully manned (*B.G.* 6.35–41).

287.

CAESAR *B.G.* 6.42 (1) On his return Caesar, who knew well enough the kinds of thing liable to happen in war, had one criticism to make: that the place should not have been left when there was even the smallest amount of risk, and the cohorts should not have been sent out from their garrison positions. In his opinion fortune had played a large part in the sudden arrival of the enemy

(2) and an even greater one in turning the barbarians aside from the very rampart and gates. (3) The most remarkable thing of all was that the Germans, who had crossed the Rhine with the intention of plundering the territory of Ambiorix, had in fact done Ambiorix the most welcome favour by turning their attention to the Roman camp.

Caesar then set out to ravage the Eburones' territory systematically; he was however unsuccessful in his attempts to capture Ambiorix.

288.

CAESAR *B.G.* 6.44 (1) After ravaging the land in this way, Caesar led back his army, now short of two cohorts, to Durocotorum [Reims] in the land of the Remi. There he called a Gallic conference and proceeded to hold an inquiry into the conspiracy of the Senones and Carnutes. (2) On Acco, the ring-leader, a rather harsh sentence was pronounced, and he was executed in the traditional manner. Those who had run away to escape punishment were outlawed. (3) Then, leaving in winter-quarters two legions near the Treveri frontier, two among the Lingones, and the remaining six at Agedincum [Sens] in the country of the Senones, he made arrangements for his army's food-supplies and then set out for his customary tour of duty in north Italy.

289.

DIO 40.32 (5) Caesar did not impose a punishment on any of the Sugambri because of the winter and political disturbances in Rome; but after deploying his soldiers into winter-quarters, he himself left for Italy, giving as his excuse his obligations in Cisalpine Gaul, but in fact to enable him to keep in close touch with what was happening in Rome.

Caesar's strategy for this year has some interesting features: the winter campaign against the Nervii; the Gallic conference called in the spring; the far-ranging demonstrations of power under divisional commanders; the reluctance to fight any open battles; the time-limit of a week (imposed for no very compelling reason); and above all the remarkable invitation issued to other tribes to join in the plunder. When this plan recoiled on Caesar's head, he blamed it on 'Fortune'. But is it likely that so experienced a commander would not have foreseen the danger? Might Caesar not have been taking a calculated risk? And if so, why was he prepared to do so? Supposing that everything had gone as he wished, Ambiorix would have been captured and the campaign completed in the early summer. What use might Caesar then have made of the rest of the year, bearing in mind the situation at Rome?

VII. The Breakdown of the Partnership

The years 52 and 51 gave Pompey his best chance of breaking away from Caesar altogether and dominating Roman politics on his own. The clamour for him to be made dictator redoubled as the new year (52) began with no magistrates to control the unprecedented violence in the streets. The murder of Clodius was only one incident among many, although it made still more remote the possibility of orthodox consular elections. Much to its credit the Senate took the initiative and, rather than allow Pompey a free hand to settle the state of emergency, subjected him to the traditional constitutional safeguards by appointing him consul — without a colleague. For a time the *optimates* were in the ascendant, and Pompey obligingly co-operated, first by refusing to renew the marriage alliance with Caesar, secondly by interfering with the arrangements which Caesar made for his political future: it was his intention to come straight from his Gallic command to a consulship in Rome without exposing himself to the danger of attack as a private citizen.

For the moment there was no possibility of Caesar leaving Gaul, where a full-scale revolt had developed under Vercingetorix. However when peace had been restored, the question of his recall was brought up again. Marcus Marcellus, one of the consuls of the following year (51), tried hard to bring matters to a head; but in the face of Caesar's tame tribunes he could do nothing without the support of Pompey. Pompey still refused to commit himself; he even talked of taking up a provincial command. In the event he decided against leaving Italy, and it must have seemed to Caesar, stamping out a few last sparks of rebellion in Gaul, that the prospect of direct confrontation with his one-time partner was now becoming a probability.

A. Pompey's sole consulship (52)

CLODIUS AND MILO

The year again started without consuls, perhaps, as some sources suggest, at Pompey's instigation. Milo was among the candidates, confident in the backing of the *optimates* and disgruntled by the constant obstructions. Opposition candidates were: Q. Caecilius Metellus Scipio, soon to become Pompey's father-in-law, and P. Plautius Hypsaeus, who had once been Pompey's quaestor in the East (Ascon. p. 35); rather improbably, they were abetted by Clodius, who saw his hopes of an influential praetorship threatened by Milo's candidature. The conflict resolved itself dramatically with Clodius' murder, removing Milo from the competition and giving rise to the state of emergency which allowed Pompey to be elected sole consul.

290.

APPIAN *B.C.* 2.20 (74) Milo, who had been of service to Pompey in facing up to Clodius and had won popular support over the recall of Cicero, thought the present anarchy was a good opportunity for seeking the consulship. But Pompey kept putting off the elections until Milo retired in disgust to his native Lanuvium, reckoning that Pompey had broken faith with him.

291.

CICERO *Mil.* 25. Clodius saw that Milo was going to be elected consul with the full consent of the Roman people and was worried by the thought that, if he were, his own praetorship would be hamstrung. So he offered his services to Milo's fellow-candidates on the condition that he could take sole charge of their campaign, whatever they said, and 'bear the whole weight of the elections on his shoulders' — that was his favourite phrase. He set about collecting tribes, acting as go-between, and making up a new Colline group from a choice collection of ruffians; but the more furiously Clodius worked, the stronger grew Milo's support. When this man who would stop at nothing saw that his bitterest enemy would, through his outstanding courage, without a doubt become consul, and realized that the people of Rome were declaring not only their approval but also their votes in his favour, then he began to bring his plans into the open and assert publicly that Milo should be killed.

26. He had brought down from the Apennines a slave-gang of loutish farm-labourers, whom he had used to ravage the public forests and terrorize Etruria. You saw them; there was absolutely no secret about it. He was constantly saying that if Milo's consulship could not be taken from him, his life could. Both

in the Senate and in public meetings he repeated the same
suggestion.

292.

ASCONIUS *in Milon.* p. 31. Milo wanted the elections completed as
soon as possible and was confident of the support both of the
optimates (a stumbling-block for Clodius) and of the people —
he had paid lavish bribes and laid out enormous sums on games,
theatrical entertainments and gladiatorial shows, which Cicero
says cost him three inheritances; his rivals were happy to put things
off and for this reason Pompey, son-in-law of Scipio, and the
tribune Titus Munatius prevented the motion being put to the
Senate that the patricians should be assembled to appoint an
interrex, even though the situation demanded one ... On Jan 19th
... Milo set out for his hometown of Lanuvium, where he was at
that time dictator, for the election of a priest on the following day.
Clodius ran into him at about three o'clock a little beyond Bovillae,
on his way back from Aricia, ... Clodius was on horse-back;
behind him were about thirty slaves, the usual sort of escort for
travellers at the time, carrying little but swords. He had three
companions with him — one a Roman Knight called Gaius Caus-
inius Schola, and two well known plebeian figures, Publius Pomponius and †Gaius Clodius†. Milo was being carried in a coach
with his wife Fausta, daughter of the dictator Sulla, and his
kinsman Marcus Fufius.

p. 32. They were followed by a large column of slaves including
a number of gladiators of whom two were well-known, Eudamus
and Birria. These men at the back of the column got into a brawl
with Clodius' slaves. When Clodius in threatening mood went
back to see what the trouble was, Birria hit him across the shoulder
with a Thracian sword. That was how the fight began. More of
Milo's men ran up. Clodius was wounded and carried into the
nearest tavern, just outside Bovillae. When Milo heard that Clodius
was wounded, he realized things would be a great deal easier for
him if Clodius died, whatever penalty he had to pay, but if he
managed to live, his own situation would be even more perilous.
So he gave orders for him to be routed out of the tavern. Marcus
Saufeius led the way; Clodius was dragged out of hiding and
finished off with repeated blows.

293.

DIO 40.48 (1) So that was the state of the city: there was no one in charge of affairs, murders were an almost daily occurrence and the magistracies remained unfilled, although in men's eagerness to win them bribery and bloodshed were resorted to. (2) Milo, one of the candidates, happened to run into Clodius on the Appian Way; at first he just wounded him, but then, for fear of repercussions, killed him . . . (3) When this news reached the city that evening, there was a fearful uproar . . . [The tribunes (Pompeius) Rufus and (Munatius) Plancus made matters worse by displaying the corpse in the forum; the people then took it up to the Senate House for cremation, but the fire was such that the building was destroyed as well] . . . 49 (5) Towards evening the Senate did finally meet on the Palatine; they decided to elect an *interrex* and to entrust the protection of the city to him, the tribunes, and furthermore to Pompey.

294.

ASCONIUS *in Milon.* p. 33. The citizens were a good deal more outraged by the burning of the Senate House than by the killing of Clodius. So Milo, who was thought already to have gone into voluntary exile, took fresh heart from the unpopularity of his opponents and returned to Rome the same night as the Senate House was burnt. Quite unabashed, he continued to campaign for the consulship and openly distributed 1,000 asses to each tribe. Some days later, the tribune Marcus Caelius convened a public meeting for him, and Cicero himself pleaded his cause to the people. Both of them said that Clodius had been the aggressor. Meanwhile *interrex* succeeded *interrex*, (p. 34) as the riotous behaviour of the candidates and the gang-warfare made it impossible to hold the consular elections. So the Senate passed a resolution that the *interrex*, the tribunes and Pompey, who had proconsular power outside the city, should see to it that no harm befell the Republic, and that Pompey should recruit from the whole of Italy.

The formula 'that no harm . . .' was the so-called 'ultimate decree' of the Senate and conferred special powers on the magistrates (cf. nos. **399** f.).

Cicero's account aimed to absolve Milo from all responsibility:

295.

CICERO *Mil.* 27. Milo was dictator at Lanuvium and had to go there on official business on Jan. 18th for the ritual election of a priest. This was common knowledge. When Clodius discovered it, he left Rome in a hurry the day before so that, as the facts later showed, he could make a surprise attack on Milo in front of his estate . . .

29. Milo ran into Clodius in front of his estate at five o'clock or thereabouts and was immediately attacked from higher ground. His coachman was stopped and killed. He himself threw off his cloak, jumped from the vehicle and began defending himself with a will. Some of Clodius' men with drawn swords ran to the coach to attack Milo from behind; others, thinking he was already dead, began cutting down the slaves who formed his rear escort. Some of these, showing great loyalty to their master in the emergency, were killed; others, seeing the fighting round the coach, tried to go to their master's assistance. They were prevented from doing so, but, hearing from Clodius' own mouth that Milo was dead and believing it to be true, they — that is, Milo's slaves; and I am not trying to take any blame off Milo, but merely state the facts — they, without orders, without the knowledge or presence of their master, did what anyone would have wanted his slaves to do in such a situation.

296.

DIO 40.50 (1) There was no end to the continual bloodshed and skirmishing. So the Senate endorsed its earlier measures and sent for Pompey, instructing him to recruit some new levies.

297.

CAESAR *B.G.* 7.1 (1) With Gaul quiet, Caesar set out for Italy to make his customary tour of duty. There he learned about Clodius' murder and, hearing that the Senate had passed a decree for calling up everyone in Italy of military age, proceeded to levy troops throughout the whole of his province.

The question whether Clodius or Milo had been the aggressor was almost irrelevant (see nos. **304–309** for the trial of Milo); far more important was the fact that both troublemakers were removed at the same time. How far reaching were the political consequences? See the rest of Section A.

THE CONSULAR ELECTIONS

It was clearly impossible that in such a crisis the state should be allowed to continue without magistrates, and the adherents of Pompey and Caesar both canvassed actively for the election of their patrons. For once however the Senate intervened and came up with the novel expedient of having one consul only, an arrangement that looked as if it would suit Senate and Pompey alike.

298.

DIO 40.50 (3) There was tremendous excitement in the city about who was to take charge; one body of opinion favoured Pompey's election as dictator, another Caesar as consul.

299.

SUETONIUS *Div. Jul.* 26 (1) Amid the general upheavals which followed Clodius' death, when the Senate had resolved that there should be only one consul, specifying Pompey, the tribunes tried to get Caesar made his colleague.

300.

PLUTARCH *Pomp.* 54 (3) The next year started without magistrates again, and there were now even more people making stronger representations about the need for a dictator. Cato and his adherents were afraid that they would have matters forcibly taken out of their hands and so decided to anticipate the possibility of the naked tyranny of a dictatorship by offering a more conventional office to Pompey. (4) And so Bibulus, in spite of being an enemy of Pompey's, made the first proposal in the Senate that Pompey should be elected sole consul . . . (5) The Senate accepted the proposal and resolved that Pompey should be elected sole consul with the option of nominating a colleague for himself, if he wanted, after a trial period of not less than three months. So Pompey was declared consul on these terms by the *interrex* Sulpicius. He acknowledged his debt to Cato and made friendly overtures to him, suggesting that he should give private advice to assist him with his office. (6) But Cato disclaimed any obligations owed to him by Pompey; he said that he had only spoken in the interests of the city, not of Pompey.

301.
VELLEIUS 2.47 (3) A third consulship was conferred on Pompey, without a colleague, at the instance of the very people who had tried to prevent his holding office before; the prestige he derived from this distinction seemed to reconcile him with the *optimates*, but it drove the deepest possible wedge between him and Caesar.

302.
DIO 40.50 (5) This sole consulship was of course unorthodox, and in fact unprecedented, and yet it looked to be the right answer: Pompey was much less favourably inclined towards the people than Caesar was, and so they hoped to be able to alienate him from the populace altogether and bring him over onto their own side. They were right: elated by this novel and unexpected honour, he ceased paying any attention to the idea of pleasing the people, but tried to carry out the will of the Senate in every detail.

Pompey does seem to have acted in the Senate's interest by passing laws intended to limit the use of violence and bribery (Ascon. p. 35); but for how long did he remain co-operative?

303.
ASCONIUS *in Milon.* p. 36. Marcus Caelius, a staunch supporter of Milo, tried to obstruct Pompey's laws, saying that there was discrimination against Milo and a precipitate rush to judgment. When he continued to voice his stubborn opposition, Pompey got so angry that he said he would use arms to defend the Republic if he were compelled to. Pompey was afraid of Milo, or at least pretended to be so; he usually stayed not in his house, but in his gardens at the upper level, where a large band of soldiers were constantly on the lookout. Once he even dismissed the Senate abruptly, saying that he was afraid of Milo coming [cf. no. **308**].

THE LAW COURTS

In one of the few of Cicero's letters that have survived from this year, he says that he is being 'kept very busy by constant action in the law courts' (*ad Fam.* 7.2.4). The results of a number of these trials are known to us, and they provide an interesting indication of the way that political influence shifted during the year.

304.

ASCONIUS *in Milon.* p. 38. A law was then passed by Pompey stipulating that the head of the board of inquiry [into Clodius' death] should be elected by popular vote from among the number of ex-consuls. Elections were at once held, and Lucius Domitius Ahenobarbus was appointed. Pompey then drew up a register of possible jurors, and people agreed that there had never been a list of people comprising such distinction and integrity.

305.

CICERO *Mil.* 22. The reason why he chose you [Domitius] above all to be in charge of this inquiry was because he wanted nothing but justice, gravity, humanity, and integrity. He resolved that only ex-consuls should be eligible, perhaps because he thought it was up to the leaders of the state to counteract the fickleness of the people and the irresponsibility of the troublemakers. But it was you he chose out of all the ex-consuls; for you had given ample proof from your earliest days of your contempt for the people's lunacy.

What was the political significance of the choice of Domitius?

306.

VELLEIUS 2.47 (4) Milo was tried and condemned, though more through the influence of Pompey than because of indignation at his action. (5) In fact Cato openly declared his opinion in favour of acquitting him.

307.

DIO 40.54 (1) The courts met without any disturbance, following these measures, and among the many convicted on various charges were Milo and others for having killed Clodius. Milo was actually defended by Cicero, (2) but the orator lost his nerve and panicked when he saw Pompey and an unusual array of soldiers in court; he could not utter a word of his prepared speech, but had difficulty getting out a few broken phrases that died on his lips and was glad to stand down. The text that we now have at hand, purporting to be the speech delivered at the time in defence of Milo, was in fact composed at leisure some time later, when he had recovered his confidence.

> How plausible does this explanation of Cicero's behaviour seem? Why else might be he have stood down?

308.

CICERO *Mil.* 67. But even if Milo is still to be feared, it is not this charge of murdering Clodius that worries us, but your suspicions, Pompey . . . If you are afraid of Milo, if you believe he is now making vicious designs on your life or has ever done anything of the kind, if the recruiting all over Italy — as some of your agents have been saying — , if these armed guards, if the cohorts on the Capitol, if the lookouts and the sentries and the young men specially picked to guard your person and your house; if all these have been drawn up, deployed and put into a state of armed readiness to withstand a lone attack from Milo, then he must have an incredible store of energy and dynamism, and strength and resources beyond the scope of any individual . . .

Milo was convicted by 38 votes to 16:

309.

ASCONIUS *in Milon.* p. 53. Of the Senators, 12 condemned and 6 acquitted; of the Knights, 13 condemned and 4 acquitted; of the Tribunes, 13 condemned and 6 acquitted. The jury seemed to accept that Clodius had been wounded initially without Milo's knowledge, but satisfied themselves that after the wounding he had been put to death on Milo's orders.

> For the 'Tribunes', see no. **243** n.

Some of the other trials during the year:

310.

DIO 40.53 (1) Among the many convicted under this new bribery law was Plautius Hypsaeus, a rival candidate of Milo and Scipio for the consulship. Although they had in fact all three been guilty of distributing bribes, he was the only one convicted. (2) Scipio had been indicted, and by two people at that, but Pompey's influence prevented the case going to court.

311.

ASCONIUS *in Milon.* p. 54. After Milo, the first to be accused under the same law of Pompey (p. 55) was Marcus Saufeius, who had taken the lead in breaking into the tavern at Bovillae and killing Clodius . . . He was defended by Cicero and Caelius, who managed to get him acquitted by one vote. He was clearly saved by the hatred attaching to Clodius, since his defence was much weaker than Milo's . . . A few days later he was again arraigned under the Violence Law of Plautius . . . but acquitted by even more votes than before . . . However Sextus Clodius, who had been responsible for having Clodius' body brought into the Senate House . . . (p. 56) . . . was condemned by the large margin of 46 votes to 5. There were many others condemned, most of them supporters of Clodius; some appeared in court to answer the charges, others were condemned in absence.

Among the Clodians convicted was the tribune T. Munatius Plancus Bursa, who had been one of the most inflammatory agitators at the time of the murder (see no. **293**).

312.

DIO 40.55 (1) Plancus was convicted in spite of the support of Pompey, who even sent to the court a leaflet containing a testimonial and an entreaty on his behalf.

Plancus retired to Ravenna, where Caesar gave him a large pension (Cic. *ad Fam.* 8.1.5, written June 51).

313.

CICERO *ad Fam.* 7.2 [Rome, c. June 52, to M. Marius] (2) I don't doubt that you are pleased about Bursa, but you are a bit cautious about congratulating me. You say that you suppose I am not at all delighted, because the man was such a poor wretch anyway. But I'd like you to know that I was more pleased by his condemnation than by my enemy's death. For I prefer victory at law to victory by the sword, and I prefer to bring credit on a friend than disaster. But what delighted me above all was the enthusiastic support given me by the *optimates* in face of unbelievable efforts made by a very distinguished and very powerful gentleman.

What evidence is there in the preceding excerpts that the *optimates* were beginning to reassert themselves?

ARRANGEMENTS FOR THE FUTURE

Even though Pompey's influence in the law courts was not unchallenged, he felt himself secure enough to resist suggestions made by Caesar of entering a second marriage alliance.

314.

SUETONIUS *Div. Jul.* 27 (1) In order to try and retain his ties of kinship and goodwill with Pompey, Caesar offered him the hand of his sister's granddaughter Octavia, even though she was already married to Gaius [Claudius] Marcellus; he himself asked to marry Pompey's daughter, although she was betrothed to Faustus Sulla.

315.

PLUTARCH *Pomp.* 55 (1) Pompey now came into the city and married Cornelia, a daughter of Metellus Scipio. It was not her first marriage, as she had just been left a widow by the death in Parthia of Publius, the son of Crassus. Apart from her youthful charms, this girl had many attractions . . . (2) But in spite of this the disparity in their ages made some critical of the marriage; Cornelia was young enough to be married to Pompey's son. (3) The more fastidious also considered that Pompey was neglecting the affairs of the ailing city which had chosen him as its cure and entrusted itself into his keeping alone; here he was engaged in wedding festivity and sacrifices when he ought to have been reflecting on the tragedy of his unconstitutional consulship which a healthy city would never have given him.

A marriage-tie might have guaranteed Pompey's co-operation, but it was not essential for Caesar's political future. His main concern was for what would happen when his provincial command came up for review. If he were compelled to return to Rome for the consular elections as a private citizen, he would be immediately vulnerable to the attacks of his enemies. To try and prevent this, he used his influence with the tribunes to have passed a law enabling him to compete for office in absence. Pompey's part in this legislation is open to question; the evidence in Cicero that he backed the tribunes' bill is non-contemporary and perhaps unhistorical. At any rate he soon neutralized it by passing a law which stipulated that candidates had to appear in person. Finally, to reinforce his own position still further, he had his Spanish command extended for another five years.

316.

DIO 40.51 (1) Pompey was however unwilling to hold office alone. Having once enjoyed the glory of being given it, he now wanted to avoid the jealousy that sprung from it. He was also afraid that if the second consulship were left vacant, then pressure from his troops and the populace might necessitate having Caesar as a colleague. (2) So in order to avoid the impression of having slighted Caesar altogether (thus giving him legitimate grounds for resentment), he arranged through the tribunes that Caesar should be allowed to compete for office in absence (provided he was entitled to it). He next chose as colleague his father-in-law Quintus Scipio, who was then under a charge of bribery . . . [see no. 310]. (3) This man had given his daughter in marriage, and now in return received from him the consulship and immunity against accusation.

317.
(From Caesar's speech to the Senate in April 49.)
CAESAR B.C. 1.32 (3) 'In the very consulship of Pompey, a law was passed allowing me to stand for the consulship in absence, in spite of the opposition of my enemies and the remorseless hostility of Cato, who in his usual way made the debate drag on for days.'

In a letter written three years later, Cicero discussed reasons why he

should or should not fight on Pompey's side in the civil war if he left
Italy:

318.

CICERO *ad Att.* 8.3. [Cales, 12 Feb. 49] (3) Now look at the
argument on the other side. Our friend Pompey has done nothing
wise, nothing brave, nothing, I might add, that was not contrary
to the weight of my advice and influence. I am not concerned with
past history, how Pompey fostered, strengthened, and armed
Caesar against the state . . . how he prolonged Caesar's provincial
command, how in Caesar's absence he helped him in everything,
how in his third consulship, when he had begun to be the defender
of the Republic, he lent weight to the proposal of the ten tribunes
that candidature in absence should be permitted, and reinforced
the point with a law of his own, how he opposed the attempts of the
consul Marcus Marcellus to terminate Caesar's Gallic commands
on March 1st [see nos. 328 ff.] — I am not concerned with all that . . .

319.

DIO 40.56 (1) Besides this he revived the law about elections,
which had become rather neglected; this stated that anyone
seeking office had to appear before the assembly and that absentee
candidates were ineligible for election. He also reinforced the
decree passed a little earlier [see no. 274] that people who had held
office in the city should only be allotted provincial commands
after an interval of five years. (2) But even after proposing these
measures, he had no compunction about taking five more years in
Spain for himself a little later, or about giving Caesar — whose
friends were terribly indignant — the right to stand for the
consulship in absence, as had been decreed. (3) For he had in fact
added to the law a clause making it legal only for people who had
had the privilege specifically conferred on them by name. This
virtually meant the same as having no law at all; for anyone with
any influence would be certain to get the privilege voted to them.

> This account is perhaps an attempt to reconcile the seeming inconsis-
> tency of Pompey's behaviour over the question of Caesar's candidature.
> But even if a rider was added, at the insistence of Caesar's friends,
> exempting him from the obligation to appear in person, it may not have
> had the status of law (see no. 320 with no. 328).

320.

SUETONIUS *Div. Jul.* 28 (3) When Pompey proposed a measure about the rights of magistrates and stipulated in one section that candidates should be debarred from seeking office in absence, he forgot to make an exception in Caesar's case; only when the law had been engraved on a bronze tablet and deposited in the treasury did he correct this omission.

Pompey's Spanish command:

321.

PLUTARCH *Caes.* 28 (5) Pompey was also voted an extension of command in his provinces; he had two, Spain and the whole of Libya, which he managed by deploying his staff and maintaining his armies there; for this he received an annual grant of 1,000 talents from the treasury.

> The period of this extension is given as four years in Plutarch *Pomp.* 55.7, five years in Dio 40.44.2, 40.56.2.

322.

APPIAN *B.C.* 2.25 (95) Although others were appointed to succeed Pompey in his office, he continued to exercise the same control and authority. Rome was completely in his hands. He had strong backing from the Senate, both because of the ill-will they bore Caesar for not consulting them at all during his consulship, and because he had set the ailing state back on its feet so rapidly without being a trouble or a trial to any of them during his year of office.

> How realistic is this estimate of Pompey's position?

Caesar had been able to exercise hardly any influence at all on Roman affairs, at a time when he most needed to in face of the domination of Pompey and the increasing confidence of the *optimates*. The Gauls were just as aware of his political preoccupations and accordingly chose this moment to revolt.

323.

CAESAR *B.G.* 7.1 (2) The news of these events quickly reached Transalpine Gaul. The Gauls themselves added to the reports and embellished them with plausible suppositions — that Caesar was detained by the disturbances in the city and, in such a time of political unrest, was unable to rejoin his army. (3) The situation added a spark of those who were already resentful of their subjection to Roman rule, and they began to make plans for rebellion with less restraint and greater audacity.

The rebel-leader who emerged was Vercingetorix, a young Arvernian chieftain. He soon won the adherence of most of the tribes in West Gaul.

324.

CAESAR *B.G.* 7.6 (1) When this news reached Caesar in Italy, he set out for Transalpine Gaul, with the knowledge that affairs in the city had reached a more stable position thanks to the influence of Pompey.

The revolt of Vercingetorix occupied Caesar's full attention for the rest of the year; almost every tribe in Gaul, including the Aedui, turned against the Romans. Caesar suffered his most substantial defeat at Gergovia, the capital of the Arverni (*B.G.* 7.37–53), and even began to withdraw towards the shelter of the Province. However a chance cavalry victory gave him back the initiative, and he brought the campaign to a triumphant conclusion by defeating Vercingetorix at his stronghold of Alesia after a monumental siege (*B.G.* 7.54–79).

325.

CAESAR *B.G.* 7.89 (5) Vercingetorix was given up, and the arms surrendered. Apart from the Aedui and Arverni captives whom he hoped to use for winning back the allegiance of their tribes, Caesar distributed all the other prisoners among his army — one to each soldier — by way of war-spoils. 90 (1) This completed, he set out into Aedui territory, and the state capitulated. (2) He also met there representatives of the Arverni promising to do as he commanded. He ordered a large number of hostages; (3) then sent his legions into winter-quarters and returned about 20,000 captives to the Aedui and Arverni.

In spite of Caesar's resounding victory it could be said that he had lost ground politically during the year both to Pompey and to the *optimates*. What indications were there that this was the case?

F

B. *The consolidation of the optimates*

THE CONSULSHIP OF MARCUS CLAUDIUS MARCELLUS (51)

The *optimates* must have been pleased with the comparative docility of Pompey the year before and the progress they had made towards restoring peaceful constitutional rule. Cato, their champion, even put himself forward for the consulship and, though he later withdrew, he would have been happy with the election of Marcellus; the other consul, Servius Sulpicius Rufus, had been one of the *interreges* who elected Pompey to his sole consulship (see no. **300**).

326.

DIO 40.58 (1) Cato had no particular desire for office, except that he could see the power of Pompey and Caesar growing beyond the bounds of the constitution, and suspected that they would either take control of affairs between them, or they would fall out and a tremendous civil war would ensue which left the victor in a monarchial position. (2) He wanted therefore to make them powerless before they could come to grips, and competed for the consulship to that end, since he would have no influence as a private citizen. But their agents suspected that he had some such design, and instead of him were elected Marcus Marcellus and Sulpicius Rufus, (3) the one because of his legal experience, the other because of his oratorical ability.

In Plutarch's account Cato seems to be acting on Pompey's behalf:

327.

PLUTARCH *Cat. Min.* 49 (1) Though Caesar himself was tied up with his armies in Gaul, he still kept up his influence in Rome by his use of gifts, money, and above all friends. By this time Cato's warnings had begun to rouse Pompey from his earlier studied indifference; but even though he had some idea of the trouble in store, he still hadn't the courage to make a decisive move to tackle and prevent it. Cato therefore launched himself into a campaign for the consulship, with the intention of depriving Caesar of his armies straightaway or charging him with conspiracy ... (3) He persuaded the Senate to pass a law that candidates for office should have to appear at the hustings in person and should not be allowed to send anyone round to canvass and make appeals on their behalf. People resented this even more, as it deprived them not only of the chance of receiving money but of bestowing favour as well. [Thereupon Cato gave up all attempts to win further office] . . . 50 (3) . . . but he said that there had been no foul play in the consular elections and he realized that it must have been his manner that offended people; no sensible person would change that to suit others, or risk similar set-backs as a result of retaining it.

The apparent end of Caesar's Gallic campaign gave fresh impetus to the question of his recall.

328.

SUETONIUS *Div. Jul.* 28 (2) The consul Marcus Claudius Marcellus, after announcing publicly that he had a radical proposition to make, brought before the Senate a motion that he should be succeeded before his time was up on the grounds that the war was over, peace had been declared, and the victorious army ought to be disbanded; he also said that Caesar should not be allowed to stand for the consulship in absence, as Pompey's subsequent measure had not superseded the decree of the people (cf. nos. **316–320**).

Were these adequate grounds for recalling Caesar? See nos. **330** f., **341** ff.

329.

APPIAN *B.C.* 2.25 (97) [When Caesar heard of Marcellus' threat] . . . the story is that he clapped his hand to the hilt of his sword and said 'This will give it to me then.'

The same story of the sword is told in Plut. *Pomp.* 58.2, except that the words are there attributed to one of Caesar's centurions who had returned to Rome and heard that Caesar's command was not to be prolonged.

330.

(CAESAR) *B.G.* 8.53 (1) The previous year, when Marcellus was trying to undermine Caesar's position, he had brought before the Senate a premature measure about dealing with Caesar's provinces contrary to the law of Pompey and Crassus; when opinions had been voiced, and Marcellus, who was doing everything to win prestige for himself and spite Caesar, was pressing for Caesar's recall, the Senate with a packed House took quite the opposite line.

The law of Pompey and Crassus, passed in 55, forbade the discussion of Caesar's provincial command until 1 March 50.

331.

DIO 40.59 (1) Marcellus, being an adherent of Pompey, at once devoted all his energies to bringing about Caesar's downfall. He introduced a number of measures to his disadvantage, including one for sending out a successor even before his stipulated time was up. There was opposition from Sulpicius and some of the tribunes who were well-disposed towards Caesar. Sulpicius sided with them and the people because he did not approve of expelling someone in the middle of his term of office when he had not done anything wrong.

Cicero was now reluctantly on his way to Cilicia whose governor he had been appointed following the law of Pompey about provincial commands (see no. **319**).

332.

CICERO *ad Att.* 5.2 [Pompeii, 10 May 51] (3) When you get back from Epirus, do please write to me about the political situation. At the moment I haven't yet got a satisfactory report of how Caesar reacted to the news of the senatorial recommendation.

The 'recommendation' was the proposal of Marcellus about Caesar's province; as it was vetoed by the tribunes, it never attained the status of a decree.

The Novum Comum incident:

333.

APPIAN *B.C.* 2.26 (98) Caesar had founded the town of Novum Comum at the foot of the Alps and given it Latin rights, which meant that Roman citizenship was conferred on the annual magistrates. One of the inhabitants who held a magistracy, and therefore considered himself a Roman, was flogged by Marcellus on some pretext or other, although Romans are immune from such punishment. But in his rage Marcellus revealed his true intention: he wanted the scars to be the mark of alien citizenship and told the man to take them away and show them to Caesar.

> There was a rumour current at the time that Caesar was going to give citizenship to all the Italians north of the Po (Cic. *ad Att.* 5.2.3). On the Latin rights see no. **335** n.

334.

SUETONIUS *Div. Jul.* 28 (3) Not content with trying to strip Caesar of his provinces and privileges, Marcellus also proposed that the colonists planted by Caesar in Novum Comum under a bill of Vatinius should be deprived of their citizenship on the grounds that it had been conferred illegally for political purposes.

335.

CICERO *ad Att.* 5.11 [Athens, 6 July 51] (2) A disgraceful perform-ance by Marcellus in the Comum affair. Even if he hadn't been a magistrate, he was still a Transpadane. So I shouldn't think it was any more popular with our friend Pompey than with Caesar. But that's his own look out.

> Cicero means that Marcellus was acting illegally if the man was a magistrate (see no. **333**), and even if not, it was an insult to Caesar, and to Pompey as well since it was probably his father who had first granted Latin rights to the towns in the area (Ascon. p. 3).

POMPEY AND SPAIN

The influence of Pompey was no longer so strongly felt in the city, and it even looked at one point as if he might go off to Spain after all. This would have saved him the embarrassment of having to declare himself over the question of Caesar's recall, but it would also have cut him off from Rome, and he could never expect to be in such a position of eminence again once Caesar was in control.

336.

(CICERO) *ad Fam.* 8.1 [Rome, June 51, from Caelius] (3) If you did bump into Pompey as you hoped, mind you send me a full account of your impressions — what he had to say to you, and what inclinations he professed (for he has a way of thinking one thing and saying another, though he is not subtle enough to conceal what he really wants).

> Before Cicero left for Cilicia, he gave instructions to Marcus Caelius Rufus, tribune in 52, to send him as much political news as possible. The series of letters written by Caelius (*ad Fam.* 8.1–14) forms a most important historical source for the years 51–50.

337.
CICERO *ad Fam.* 2.8 [Athens, 6 July 51, to Caelius] (2) I have spent several days with Pompey, talking nothing but politics; but I cannot — and should not — repeat in writing what we said. I will just say that Pompey is an exceptional person, psychologically prepared to take any strategic steps necessary for the welfare of the state.

> Compare this judgement on Pompey with that made by Caelius in no. **336.** How should we assess Pompey's behaviour during the year? Can any consistent principles be observed? See also no. **343** n.

338.
CICERO *ad Att.* 5.11 [Athens, 6 July 51] (3) You say it is Varro's opinion that Pompey will go to Spain. I certainly think so, though I don't approve of the idea at all: in fact I found it quite easy to persuade Theophanes that the best policy was for Pompey to stay in Rome. So the Greek will press him to do so, and he has very considerable influence with him.

> Varro was one of Pompey's legates in Spain.

339.
CICERO *ad Fam.* 3.8 [Cilicia, 8 Oct., to Ap. Claudius Pulcher] (10) I would be grateful if you could write to me as often as possible about anything that concerns you or me; and about the political situation in general, which worries me all the more because of the information in your letter that Pompey is about to go to Spain.

> Appius had been Cicero's predecessor as governor of Cilicia.

340.

DIO 40.59 (2) Pompey had left the city as if to go and campaign in Spain, but in fact he did not leave Italy even on this occasion; instead he left the whole Spanish business to his subordinates, while he himself brooded over the city.

PROVINCIAL COMMANDS

Marcellus had failed in his first attempt to get Caesar recalled; the reaction of the tribunes had shown that optimate pressure on its own was not enough to get the measure through. The only hope seemed to lie in Pompey and when he returned to Rome in July, ostensibly on his way to Spain, the question was reopened.

341.

(CICERO) *ad Fam.* 8.4 [Rome, 1 Aug. 51, from Caelius] (4) I had given up expecting anything new on the political front when the Senate met in the temple of Apollo on July 22nd; they were discussing the question of pay for Pompey's troops, when the matter of the legion he had lent to Caesar was raised (cf. no. **282**) — whose it was, and how long he was going to let it stay in Gaul. After some hesitation Pompey, under pressure from the abuse of his critics, was forced to agree to recall it. Then he was asked about Caesar's successor; relating to this question of provincial commands, a resolution was passed 'that Pompey should return to the city straightaway so that the business of choosing successors to the provinces could be debated in his presence.' Pompey was in fact just on the point of joining his army at Ariminum — and indeed did so immediately afterwards. I think the business will be decided on August 13th. Either some definite step will be taken, or there will be a shameless use of the veto. For in the course of the debate Pompey made this sententious utterance: 'Everyone ought to respect the pronouncements of the Senate.'

In fact the issue of the provinces hung fire for two months as various technicalities prevented the Senate meeting in sufficient numbers.

342.

(CICERO) *ad Fam.* 8.9 [Rome, 2 Sept. 51, from Caelius] (2) The provinces, I told you, would be dealt with on August 13th; but the trial of [Gaius Claudius] Marcellus, the consul designate, has got in the way. The matter was adjourned to September 1st, but they couldn't even get a quorum in the House. I'm writing this on September 2nd, but so far no real progress has been made. As I see it, the whole thing will be put off till next year, and my guess is that you will have to leave someone behind to look after your province. We are getting nowhere with the succession problem as the Gauls are being put in the same category as the other provinces, and any suggestion of transferring them is vetoed ... (5) Your friend Pompey openly asserts the impossibility of Caesar holding a province and †being† consul at the same time. What he gave as his opinion in the Senate however was that no resolution should be passed at the present moment. Scipio's proposal was that the Gallic provinces should be discussed on March 1st, and nothing else. This caused considerable distress to Cornelius Balbus and I know he had words with Scipio about it.

The Scipio referred to was Pompey's father-in-law.
For Balbus, see no. 186 n.

The debate was not finally held until the very end of September.

343.
(CICERO) *ad Fam.* 8.8 [Rome, Oct. 51, from Caelius] (4) There has been absolutely no action on the political front for some days, as people are waiting to see what will be done about the Gallic provinces. The matter was often gravely discussed and then shelved; but finally when it had been established that Pompey was in favour of Caesar leaving his province after March 1st, a decree of the Senate was passed, which I send you, together with the resolutions recorded:

(5) 'Decree and Resolutions of the Senate. Sept. 29th in the Temple of Apollo. Present were: L. Domitius Ahenobarbus, Q. Caecilius Metellus, L. Villius Annalis, C. Septimius, C. Lucilius Hirrus, C. Scribonius Curio, L. Ateius Capito, M. Eppius. Whereas M. Marcellus, consul, raised the matter of the provinces to be assigned to ex-consuls, it was resolved as follows: L. Paullus and C. Marcellus, consuls, when they have entered office, shall, after the first day of March that falls within their

magistracy, bring the matter of the consular provinces before the Senate, and shall not, after the first of March, give precedence to any other matter . . . There was no veto.

(6) Sept. 30th in the Temple of Apollo; [other preamble as above]. . . . it was resolved as follows; that it is the opinion of the Senate that if any have the power to impose a veto or other hindrance, they should not bring about a delay which might prevent any matter concerning the Republic and People from being brought before the Senate, or any resolution being passed. If any shall impose a veto on this decree of the Senate, it is the wish of the Senate that a resolution be drafted and the matter be referred to the Senate and People at the earliest opportunity. This decree was vetoed by C. Caelius, L. Vinicius, P. Cornelius, C. Vibius Pansa, tribunes of the people.

(7) That it is also the wish of the Senate concerning the soldiers in the army of C. Caesar, that those of them who have served their full time or have a case for being dismissed, should be referred to this House in order that their claims may be heard and their cases recognized. If any shall impose a veto . . . [etc. as in (6) above] . . . This decree was vetoed by C. Caelius and C. Pansa, tribunes of the people.'

(8) . . . [a decree about the praetorian provinces, also vetoed by Caelius and Pansa.]

(9) There were also some remarks of Pompey's which gave considerable grounds for hope; he said that he could not reasonably decide about Caesar's provinces before March 1st, but would not hesitate to do so after that date. When asked what would happen if anyone imposed a veto on that day, he said it made no difference whether Caesar intended to disobey the Senate's decree, or to put up someone else to prevent the Senate passing a decree. 'What then if he wants to be consul and retain his army?' said another. Pompey very mildly replied 'What if my son wanted to lay into me with a cudgel?' By remarks like these he led people to believe that there was something between him and Caesar. So now it looks to me as if Caesar means to plump for one of these two alternatives: either he will stay in his province and forfeit his candidature this year, or he will leave it if he can be designated consul first. (10) Curio is preparing to make an all-out attack on him, but I don't know what he can gain by it. But he has got the

right ideas and, even if nothing comes of it, his efforts won't be wasted. I myself am treated very generously by Curio, and he has put me under some obligation by his services.

> The resolution in (7) seems to be an attempt to deprive Caesar of some of his soldiers.
>
> What was Pompey's attitude? Was his 'very mild' tone ironical? What was the meaning of the remark about the cudgel? The Latin is unfortunately ambiguous: the phrase 'something between' is a translation of the word *negotium*, which could mean either 'trouble' or 'arrangement'. Caelius in fact uses the same word in (10) of his own relations with Curio: 'he has imposed a *negotium* on me by his services.'

Cicero himself had other preoccupations: he had left for Cilicia with extreme reluctance as he was afraid both that he might get involved in a major war with the Parthians and that events in Rome might prevent a successor being sent out. In mid-September a large Parthian army crossed the Euphrates (Cic. *ad Att.* 5.18.1, *ad Fam.* 15.1.2 — an official despatch to the Senate); this new threat increased Cicero's anxiety not to have his command prolonged and gave rise to the suggestion that Pompey might succeed him.

344.

(CICERO) *ad Fam.* 8.10 [Rome, 17 Nov. 51, from Caelius] (2) The news of the Parthians' crossing has given rise to all sorts of suggestions. One idea is that Pompey should be sent, another that he should not be dispatched from Rome, another that Caesar should go with his army, another that the consuls should handle it; but no one approves of the idea that non-magistrates be sent by special decree of the Senate. (3) The year is ending (I'm writing this on Nov. 17th), and it is evident that nothing can be done before Jan. 1st. You know Marcellus — how slow and ineffectual he is, and what a procrastinator Servius is ... When the new magistrates take office, their hands will be full for the first few months if there's a Parthian war; if there is no such war, or just one small enough for you or your successors to handle with a few extra forces, I can see Curio killing two fine birds with one stone — by taking something from Caesar and bestowing some office, no matter how tiny, on Pompey.

In fact events compelled Cicero to take the initiative and he won a very creditable victory. He defeated the Parthians in open battle on Oct. 13th (for which he was hailed as *Imperator* by his troops) and ended the year by capturing the enemy fortress of Pindenissus (Cic. *ad Att.* 5.20, *ad Fam.* 2.10).

CAESAR'S CAMPAIGNS IN 51

If Caesar had any thoughts of returning to Italy to contest the elections, he must have changed his mind at once in view of the open hostility of Marcus Marcellus. In Gaul he could expect no more serious resistance, but there were just enough pockets of rebellion left to keep his soldiers occupied without overtaxing them after the rigours of eighteen months of continuous fighting.

345.

(CAESAR) *B.G.* 8.1 (1) The whole of Gaul had now been conquered, and Caesar wanted his soldiers to recover quietly in winter-quarters from the exertions of a campaign which had lasted continuously from the previous summer. But reports came in of conspiracies being made to renew the war by several states at the same time. (2) A plausible reason suggested for this was that all the Gauls realized that they could not match the Romans in a full-scale encounter of their combined forces, but if several states staged simultaneous outbreaks at different places, the Romans would not have the support or breadth of resources to be able to deal with them all.

In Jan. 51 Caesar marched into the territory of the Bituriges and by a show of strength and clemency secured their future loyalty (*B.G.* 8.2–3).

346.

(CAESAR) *B.G.* 8.4 (1) As a reward for the efforts and resilience of his soldiers, who had stuck rigorously to their task in spite of the wintry conditions, with very taxing marches and intolerable cold, Caesar promised each of his men 200 sesterces and †a thousand† to each centurion, in lieu of spoils.

Caesar next forestalled trouble from the Carnutes (*B.G.* 8.4–5); then marched against the formidable Bellovaci with four legions. Their resistance compelled him to send for three more, and he had substantial casualties but in a decisive battle was finally victorious (*B.G.* 8.6–20).

347.

(CICERO) *ad Fam.* 8.1 [Rome, June 51, from Caelius] (4) About Caesar there's no shortage of rumours, none of them very nice; at any rate we have whisperers among us; one says that he has lost his cavalry — which I don't doubt; another that the Seventh Legion has taken a beating; that he himself is blockaded by the Bellovaci and cut off from the rest of his army; as yet there is nothing definite, and even these suspicions are not being broadcast in public, but are being passed round as an open secret among a small circle of your acquaintances.

348.

(CAESAR) *B.G.* 8.24 (1) After the suppression of the most dangerous tribes, Caesar saw that there was no other state likely to put up armed resistance; but as there was considerable migration away from the towns and cultivated regions to avoid coming under the new regime, he decided to deploy his army over a wider area. (2) He kept with him his quaestor Marcus Antonius with the 12th legion, but sent the legionary commander Gaius Fabius with 25 cohorts to the most westerly part of Gaul (he had heard that there were some states up in arms in those parts and did not think the two legions under Gaius Caninius Rebilus were strong enough). (3) He also summoned Titus Labienus with the 15th legion which he had been keeping in winter-quarters and sent him to Cisalpine Gaul to look after the colonies of Roman citizens there, in case they should suffer the same sort of trouble from barbarian raids as had befallen Tergeste the year before.

> It is possible that Caesar was not only thinking of the military situation when he despatched this legion over the Alps; see nos. **333** ff., **350** f.

While Caesar ravaged the territory of the Eburones, his lieutenants conducted successful operations against the Andes (*B.G.* 8.24–29, 31). Then news came of a more serious outbreak instigated by the Senones and Cadurci who occupied the stronghold of Uxellodunum (*B.G.* 8.30, 32–38). Caesar thought this worthy of his personal attention.

349.

(CAESAR) *B.G.* 8.39 (2) Caesar thought the enemy's numbers insignificant, but decided nonetheless that their obstinacy would have to be severely punished; he did not want the whole of Gaul to imagine that it just needed perseverance, not strength, to resist the Romans, and the other states to follow their example in making a bid for freedom. The situation favoured them, (3) as it was known by all the Gauls that he only had one more summer in command of the province, and, unless he were able to retain it, the danger would be over.

The town surrendered soon after Caesar's arrival, but he decided to make an example of the inhabitants by cutting off the hands of all those engaged in the fighting (*B.G.* 8.40–44). Meanwhile Labienus was successful in his operations against the Treveri, and Caesar finished the year with a tour of Aquitania before settling the troops in winter-quarters that spanned the whole of Gaul: four legions in Belgium, two with the Aedui, two with the Turoni, two with the Lemovici. He himself wintered at Nemetocenna (Arras) (*B.G.* 8.45–46).

VIII. The Onset of Civil War

The prospect of peaceful settlement was as remote as ever when the new year (50) opened. None of the parties involved was prepared to give ground: Pompey refused to take up a provincial command, while Caesar refused to lay down his until his election as consul had been assured; the *optimates* were determined that Caesar should be recalled, while the Caesarian tribunes vetoed every attempt to achieve it. Caesar himself was better placed than he had been for some years; the situation was such that now, after a peaceful winter, he could afford to devote all his energies to politics. As well as making a triumphal tour of Cisalpine Gaul, he used his agents to buy the support of people at Rome who had influence, whether constitutional or not.

These were certainly the ingredients of civil war, but to say that they made its outbreak inevitable is no more than to say that war occurred. From Cicero's letters it appears that, as the year progressed, even the *optimates* were prepared to make concessions to Caesar in the interests of preserving the peace; Caesar too gave every appearance of preferring a diplomatic settlement. Why then was armed conflict not avoided?

A. The ending of Caesar's command

CAESAR'S CANVASS FOR SUPPORT

Caesar used his money and prestige to win support in north Italy and particularly in Rome. Some of this was to secure the immediate co-operation of the magistrates of the year, some to ensure that the magistrates for the next year (49) were favourable, and some to provide him with a strong body of sympathizers when he came to seek office himself.

350.
(CAESAR) *B.G.* 8.50 (1) At the conclusion of winter Caesar, contrary to his usual practice, set out for Italy with all possible speed to canvass the boroughs and colonies to whom he had entrusted the campaign of his quaestor, Marcus Antonius, for the priesthood. (2) He was happy to devote his energies to the support

of a man so closely allied to him (he had sent him on to present his candidature a little beforehand) and a further stimulus was provided by the opposition of the strong oligarchic faction who wished to discredit Caesar as he left his province by rejecting Antonius . . . 51 (1) Caesar's arrival was the signal for a remarkable demonstration of esteem and affection from all the boroughs and colonies. (2) It was his first visit since his campaign against united Gaul, and every conceivable device was used to decorate the gates, roads, and places on his route . . . 52 (1) When Caesar had completed his tour of the whole of Cisalpine Gaul, he returned with all speed to his army at Nemetocenna; the legions were all called out from their winter-quarters to join him in the territory of the Treveri where he reviewed the army. (2) He put Labienus in charge of Cisalpine Gaul, to ensure even stronger support for his consular candidature. He then began travelling just enough to ensure good health by change of situation. (3) On the way he received constant reports that his enemies were getting at Labienus and there was a small faction working to deprive him of a part of his army with the authority of the Senate (see nos. **369** ff.). But he did not pay attention to the rumour about Labienus and could not be persuaded to do anything which would contravene the Senate's authority. He imagined that he would have no difficulty in getting what he wanted by the open votes of the Senators.

351.

SUETONIUS *Div. Jul.* 26 (3) If there were any notable gladiators who failed to win the favour of the spectators in their fights, Caesar had them forcibly removed and kept for his own service. He had his novices trained, not in the Arms School under professional trainers but in private houses under Roman Knights or even Senators who were experienced in weapon-drill, and, as his letters show, he was desperately anxious that they would personally undertake individual tuition and supervise the exercises themselves. Caesar also doubled the legionary pay as a permanent measure; he made unlimited distributions of grain whenever there was plenty and from time to time gave every man a slave apiece out of those he had captured . . . 28 (1) He took just as much trouble trying to win the support of kings and provinces all over the world; to some he gave thousands of captives as a present; to others he sent help, wherever and whenever it was wanted, regardless of the recommendations of the Senate and People; besides this he lavished superb public buildings on the principal cities of Italy, the Gallic and Spanish provinces, Asia and Greece.

> Dio 40.60.3–4 includes slaves, Knights and Senators among his supporters.

Even Cicero was under a financial obligation:

352.
CICERO *ad Att.* 5.6 [Tarentum, 19 May 51] (2) One request I shall continue to make so long as I think you are in town is that you should settle the matter of my debt to Caesar.

353.
CICERO *ad Att.* 7.8 [Formiae, 25/26 Dec. 50] (5) The most tiresome thing for me is that I have got to spend on repaying Caesar the money that ought to be going towards my triumph. It's bad form to be in debt to a political opponent.

The magistrates of 50:

354.
APPIAN *B.C.* 2.26 (100) So for the following year [50] the bitterest enemies of Caesar were chosen as consuls — Aemilius Paullus and [Gaius] Claudius Marcellus, cousin of the other Marcellus [consul of 51]; and as tribune Curio, who was also fiercely opposed to Caesar, but had great skill as a speaker and was very popular with the people. (101) Caesar could make no impression on Claudius with his money, but he bought for 1,000 talents a promise from Paullus not to take either side, and with an even larger sum he purchased the assistance of Curio, whom he knew to be burdened with considerable debts. (102) With this money Paullus dedicated to the Roman people a particularly beautiful Basilica which was called after him.

> There is also a tradition, reported in Dio 40.59.4, that the two Marcelli were brothers; Gaius was related to Caesar by marriage, having married Caesar's great-niece (see no. **314**).

THE TRIBUNATE OF CURIO

When Curio was elected to the tribunate, his sympathies were supposed to lie with the *optimates*; but this was a matter of convenience rather than conviction, and he was readily persuaded to change sides.

355.

CICERO *ad Fam.* 8.4 [Rome, 1 Aug. 51, from Caelius] (2) I don't suppose you were surprised to hear of the conviction of Servaeus, the tribune-elect; his place is sought by Gaius Curio, which makes those familiar with his flighty nature very apprehensive. I just hope he carries on the way he is going now and continues to side with the Senate and *optimates*. At the moment his enthusiasm for them bubbles over. This attitude springs from an occasion when Caesar, who makes a practice of attaching to himself the support of the lowest elements, regardless of cost, insulted him deeply. In fact the whole thing seems to have fallen out very nicely; I am not the only one to have remarked that, for all his impulsiveness, Curio seems to have had some deep-laid motives for not heeding the advice of those who set themselves against his tribunate.

356.

(CICERO) *ad Fam.* 2.7 [Pindenissus, Nov./Dec. 51, to Curio, now tribune] (4) When I was with you and had no idea that you were going to be a tribune of the people for this coming year, I made a request which I often repeated in my letters . . . not that any new decrees should be passed (a difficult matter anyway on the whole) but that nothing new should be decreed; and that you should protect the authority and the laws of the Senate, so that I might find the situation unchanged on my return.

> Cicero also wrote to both consuls elect, *ad Fam.* 15.12 to Paullus, *ad Fam.* 15.7 to Gaius Marcellus, not only to congratulate them but also to ask that his own year of office should not be extended.

Curio's first legislation, an attack on the law passed by Caesar in 59 to help Pompey, seemed to be aimed against both of them.

357.

(CICERO) *ad Fam.* 8.10 [Rome, 17 Nov. 51, from Caelius] (4) There's one other thing to add to Curio's activities — his proposal about the Campanian land; they say that Caesar is not bothered by it, but Pompey objects most strongly, as he doesn't want it left unoccupied for Caesar when he comes home.

For the earlier legislation, see nos. 18 ff.

At some time during the winter, Curio changed allegiance.

358.

VELLEIUS 2.48 (3) Of all the sparks which ignited the civil war and the twenty years of continuous evils that ensued, none was greater than the tribune Gaius Curio; he was a man of noble birth, eloquent and outspoken, who regarded everyone's money and morals as equally expendable, a plausible rogue with a remarkable genius for doing harm, (4) and an insatiable appetite for sensual and financial gratification. To begin with he was on Pompey's side, in other words, as was then imagined, on the side of the Republic; but then he pretended to oppose both Pompey and Caesar, while in fact sympathizing with Caesar. Whether this was in fact due to a simple change of mind or to a gift of 100,000 sesterces, as I have heard rumoured, I shall leave you to decide.

Was Velleius right to assign such importance to Curio? See nos. 362–6, 374, 381, 383, 387, 390.

359.

APPIAN *B.C.* 2.27 (102) As Curio did not want to be caught changing sides too suddenly, he introduced plans for repairing and building roads on an enormous scale, appointing himself as the overseer for five years. He knew that no such proposal would be approved but hoped that Pompey's friends would oppose it, thus giving him grounds for complaint against Pompey. (103) Things turned out as he had expected and duly provided him with a pretext for disagreement.

See also the similar account in Dio 40.61.

360.

(CICERO) *ad Fam.* 8.6 [Rome, Feb. 50, from Caelius] (5) I said earlier in this letter that Curio was having a chilly time of it; well, he's in a hot spot now all right. He's being pulled to pieces and roasted. For the most trivial reason — because he had failed to get an intercalary month inserted — he has crossed over onto the popular side and begun speaking up for Caesar.

Cicero, writing back in May (*ad Fam.* 2.13.3), said that he had expected the change.

The intercalary month, to bring the months back into line with the lunar calendar, would normally be inserted after Feb. 23rd, and so would have postponed for a month the debate on the provinces scheduled for March 1st.

THE DEBATE ON THE PROVINCES

The date to which everyone had been looking was March 1st, fixed five years earlier as the day after which negotiations could start for appointing a successor to Caesar (cf. nos. **330, 342**). As his advocate, Curio insisted simply that if Caesar's command was to be terminated, Pompey too must be deprived of his army and province, even though there was no question of his period of command having expired. To many people, including a majority of the Senate, this seemed an equitable compromise, but it was never adopted. (For discussion about the terminal date of Caesar's command, see Bibliography.)

361.

CICERO *ad Att.* 5.20 [Cilicia, late Dec. 51] (7) Fancy your not being in Rome! Everything depends on what happens on March 1st. What I'm afraid is that, when the question of the provinces is discussed, Caesar may resist and I shall be kept in office. But if you could be there, I should have no fears.

Cicero was still hoping that Pompey would succeed to the command against the Parthians if not prevented by fear of Caesar.

362.

CICERO *ad Att.* 6.2 [Laodicea, May 50] (6) I have got the city Gazette up to March 7th; I see from it that our friend Curio, by his persistence, has had the provincial question put last on the agenda.

The Gazette: in his consulship Caesar had enacted that all the proceedings of the Senate should be made public; Suet. *Div. Jul.* 20.1.

When the debate was finally opened, the consul Gaius Claudius Marcellus made the initial attack.

363.

APPIAN *B.C.* 2.27 (103) Claudius proposed the sending of successors to take over Caesar's provinces as his term of command was ending. Paullus said nothing. (104) Curio thought fit to differ from both and while applauding Claudius' proposal added the rider that Pompey ought to give up his army and his provinces in the same way as Caesar; this way he said the government of the country would retain its integrity and there would be nothing to fear from any quarter. (105) The idea was widely opposed as unjust since Pompey's term of office had not expired. This brought from Curio a plain, unequivocal contention that no successors should be sent to replace Caesar, unless Pompey were replaced as well. They were so suspicious of each other, he said, that the peace of the country could not be guaranteed unless they were both out of office. He knew of course that Pompey would not give up his command, and he could see how unpopular Pompey was with the people because of his prosecutions for bribery. (106) But Curio himself was applauded by the people because his proposition looked very reasonable and because they thought he alone had been prepared to incur the enmity of both men, in duty to the state.

Curio's proposal is also reported in *B.G.* 8.52.4–5, and Dio 40.62.3. Is it likely to have been made in good faith or not?

364.

DIO 40.62 (4) The reason for making this proposal was not because he was in favour of Caesar accepting the first alternative, but because he knew perfectly well that Pompey would reject it; and this gave Caesar a plausible excuse for not dismissing his soldiers either.

The only concession that came out of the debate was quite worthless for Caesar, as it implicitly excluded him from the elections of the current year and left him unprotected in 49:

365.

(CICERO) *ad Fam.* 8.11 [Rome, April 50, from Caelius] (3) As far as the political situation is concerned, the whole argument boils down to one issue — the question of the provinces; so far Pompey has come down on the side of the Senate, that Caesar should leave his command on Nov. 13th. But that is the last thing Curio will tolerate ... I tell you this: if they squash Curio at every turn, Caesar will defend the right of veto. If, as looks likely, they are afraid to do anything about him, Caesar will stay on as long as he pleases.

The debate continued, and in June even swung a little in Caesar's favour when Pompey fell ill and the Senate agreed to uphold Curio's veto rather than commit themselves to the extreme line of Gaius Marcellus.

366.

(CICERO) *ad Fam.* 8.13 [Rome, June 50, from Caelius] (2) You will be glad to hear that Curio's veto on the provincial question ended triumphantly. The matter of the veto was raised (in accordance with a senatorial decree) and the first person to give his opinion was Marcus Marcellus, who said that something should be done with the tribunes of the people; but a packed House went firmly against the idea. I tell you though, the Great Pompey is so listless at the moment that he can scarcely make up his mind what he does want.

There is a more explicit reference to Pompey's illness in Cic. *ad Att.* 6.3.4, also written in June.

POMPEY AND THE PARTHIAN LEGIONS

The illness proved transient, and Pompey was greeted with redoubled enthusiasm when he returned. He even scored a trick off Caesar by taking back the legion he had recently lent (see no. **282**), when the Senate began conscripting for a new Parthian campaign. Caesar paid them well before they left, but they still found their way into Pompey's hands at the end of the year, when the Parthian trouble proved not to be urgent.

367.

CICERO *Tusc.* 1 (86) Our friend Pompey fell seriously ill at Naples, but he recovered. The people of Naples — and naturally of Puteoli as well — put garlands on their heads, and public congratulations came pouring in from other towns.

According to Plutarch *Pomp.* 57.1–3 these celebrations so turned
Pompey's head that he had nothing but contempt for Caesar's power
thereafter. What evidence is there in the following excerpts to suggest
that this was so? See no. **388**.

368.

APPIAN *B.C.* 2.28 (107) From his sick-bed in Italy Pompey sent
a cleverly phrased letter to the Senate, paying tribute to Caesar's
achievements and listing his own; he said that he had been given
his third consulship and after it a provincial command with an
army; he had not deliberately sought them, but had accepted them
in return for his services to the state; 'and what I was unwilling to
take', he said, 'I will happily give up to anyone who wants them,
without waiting for the terminal date of the command.' (108) The
ingenious thing about the letter was that it gave credit to Pompey
while casting a slur on Caesar, who was showing no signs of giving
up his command even after it had officially expired. When Pompey
returned to the city, he repeated what he had said in the letter and
promised then and there to lay down his command. He also said
that Caesar would be happy to lay down his as well in deference to
the ties of friendship and kinship; (109) Caesar's campaign had
been long and arduous against the fiercest fighters, and now, after
greatly extending the empire, he would come back to relax with
his honours and his sacrificial duties. In saying this he intended that
Caesar should be replaced straightaway, while he himself was
bound only in word. (110) But Curio attacked him for this sophistry;
he said that a promise was not enough; he must disarm immediately,
as there was no cause for disbanding Caesar's army until he himself became a private citizen again.

369.

(CAESAR) *B.G.* 8.54 (1) There was then a senatorial decree that
Gnaius Pompey and Gaius Caesar should each contribute a
legion for the Parthian campaign; but this was a blatant artifice to
get two legions from the same man. (2) For Pompey treated as his
own the first legion which had been given to Caesar, in whose
province it was raised, and offered that. (3) Caesar knew exactly
what was going on in the minds of his opponents, but still sent the
legion back to Pompey and in his own name ordered the 15th

legion, which he had stationed in Nearer Gaul, to be handed over
in accordance with the senatorial decree.

According to Appian *B.C.* 2.29 (114) Caesar gave each man a bounty
of 250 drachmae before he was sent back.

370.

APPIAN *B.C.* 2.30 (115) As there was no sign of trouble in Syria,
these legions spent the winter [50/49] in Capua. (116) The men sent
by Pompey to Caesar to take command of them started spreading
bad reports about Caesar; they assured Pompey that Caesar's
troops were exhausted by the rigours of the long campaign,
longed for their homeland and would come over onto his side as
soon as they crossed the Alps. (117) They may have spoken like
that either in ignorance or because they had been bribed to do so,
but in fact every man was a staunch supporter of Caesar and
prepared to do anything for him. Such was the influence of
military discipline and of the profits which war brings to the
victors and which Caesar likewise distributed; he spared no
expense to win their support for his designs. They knew themselves
what he planned, but stayed by him none the less.

This supposed disaffection among Caesar's troops is also reported in
Plut. *Pomp.* 57.4.

371.

DIO 40.66 (1) The legions which had been made ready with a view
to being sent against the Parthians proved to be redundant; and
so Marcellus, who was afraid that they would be given back to
Caesar, declared that they were needed in Italy and, as I have said,
entrusted them to Pompey. (2) This happened towards the end of
the year and did not look likely to remain valid for long as it had
not been formally approved either by the Senate or the people. So
Marcellus won over to Pompey's side the consuls due to enter
office next year, Cornelius Lentulus and Gaius Claudius, and had
them endorse the same arrangements (3) Those elected to magistracies are allowed to issue proclamations and perform various
other functions connected with their office even before they have
officially entered it, and so they thought they were entitled to do

this as well. As for Pompey, although he was normally punc-
tilious, yet on this occasion, because of his need for soldiers, he
did not go out of his way to find out where they came from or how
they came into his hands, but accepted them with wholehearted
gratitude.

> Care must be taken not to confuse the Gaius Claudius Marcellus
> elected as consul for 49 (see also nos. **375, 401**) with the consul of 50
> who has the same name.

Caesar himself saw this retention of the legions as an inducement to war.

372.

(CAESAR) *B.G.* 8.55 (1) When Caesar arrived in Italy, he discovered that the legions he had released had been handed over to
Pompey by the consul Gaius Marcellus and were being kept in
Italy, although according to the decree of the Senate they ought to
have been on their way to fight the Parthians. (2) This action left no
doubt in anyone's mind what steps were being taken against
Caesar; but he was still determined not to be drawn, so long as any
chance remained of settling the matter legally by negotiations
rather than by resorting to arms ... [Here the Commentaries end.]

373.

CAESAR *B.C.* 1.4 (4) Pompey, goaded by Caesar's enemies and his
own reluctance to allow anyone else to rival his position of prestige,
broke off all ties of friendship with Caesar and went back to
supporting their common enemies — most of whom he had
himself imposed on Caesar at the time of their link through
marriage; (5) at the same time he was sensitive of the discredit he
had incurred by diverting the legions bound for Asia and Syria
to the furtherance of his own power and position, and was anxious
to resolve the matter by the declaration of war.

THE MAGISTERIAL ELECTIONS

Caesar's attempts to win friendly magistrates were only partially successful. As censor for the year, his father-in-law was a disappointment, and
neither of the consuls could be expected to be sympathetic. But he had
another helpful tribune in Antony, who also gave him personal satisfaction

by winning the augurate from Domitius. Caelius records Domitius' fury in (Cic.) *ad Fam.* 8.14.1.

374.

DIO 40.63 (2) Caesar had a large number of supporters including Lucius Paullus (Marcellus' colleague in the consulship) and his father-in-law Lucius Piso [cons. 58], who, albeit against his will, had just been made censor with Appius Claudius [cons. 54]. (3) So Caesar had him on his side by virtue of the family tie; he was also considerably helped, though not intentionally, by Claudius who was really an opponent as he favoured Pompey [cf. (Cic.) *ad Fam.* 8.6.3]. For Claudius, overriding his colleague's objections, struck off a very large number of Knights and Senators, and so drove them all into the arms of the Caesarian faction . . . (5) When Curio was also about to have his name struck off, Piso managed to prevent it with the help of Paullus to whom he was related.

64 (1) So Appius Claudius did not succeed in getting rid of him, but he still made a speech in the Senate to publicize what he thought of him. Curio was so infuriated by this that he set upon Appius and tore his clothes. At once [Gaius] Marcellus arrested him and set about putting his case to the vote, as he thought the Senators would pass some stringent decree against him, which would also militate against Caesar. (2) At first Curio objected to the idea of any vote being taken against himself, but then when he realized that the majority of the Senators then present either actively supported Caesar's cause, or else were thoroughly afraid of him, he left it to them to decide, (3) . . . So Marcellus, completely confident of a conviction, brought a charge against him; when the majority in fact acquitted him, (4) Marcellus was so upset that he rushed from the Senate House and went straight to Pompey who was then in the suburbs. Then on his own initiative, without any official vote, he entrusted to Pompey the protection of the city with two legions of citizen-troops (cf. no. **381**).

375.

(CAESAR) *B.G.* 8.50 (3) In fact he heard that Antony had been made augur while still on his way to Italy, but still thought he had as good a reason for going round the boroughs and colonies, to thank them for rallying to Antony's support; (4) at the same time he wanted to draw their attention to himself as a suitable candidate for office the following year, especially as his opponents were rudely boasting that they had elected as consuls Lucius Lentulus and Gaius [Claudius] Marcellus who would strip Caesar of every office and rank, and they had kept Servius Galba out of the office, although he had potentially more votes and support because of the connection with Caesar forged by the close links of his legionary command.

376.

PLUTARCH *Ant.* 5 (1) Curio, the friend of Antony, changed over onto Caesar's side and brought Antony with him. He had great influence with the people because of his powers of speaking, and, with the further assistance of lavish expenditure of funds supplied by Caesar, he secured for Antony the tribunate and later the priesthood which they call the augurate. (2) As soon as Antony entered office, he gave substantial help to those campaigning on behalf of Caesar. First, when the consul Marcellus wanted to hand over to Pompey the soldiers already collected and give him the power to recruit others besides, he opposed the idea and drafted an edict that the troops already collected should sail to Syria to help Bibulus in his war against the Parthians, and that Pompey should not be allowed to keep the troops he was then levying.

To the *optimates* it came as a shock when some of the least expected magistrates apparently took Caesar's side. Bribery may well have been involved.

377.

CICERO *ad Att.* 6.8 [Ephesus, 1 Oct. 50] (1) Just as I had taken up my pen to write to you, Batonius arrived at my Ephesus home having come straight from his ship with your letter of Sept. 29th ... (2) He brought quite terrible news about Caesar, which he amplified in talking to Lepta; I just hope it's untrue, but it's certainly very frightening — that he won't dismiss his army under any circumstances, that the elected praetors and tribune Cassius and consul Lentulus are siding with him, and that Pompey is thinking of leaving the city.

CAESAR'S PREPARATIONS

In spite of the fact that Curio had managed to prevent the passage of legislation which removed Caesar from his command, neutral observers could see no prospect but war. There could be no resolution unless either of the protagonists gave ground, Pompey by going to a province, Caesar by leaving one.

378.

(CICERO) *ad Fam.* 8.14 [Rome, Aug. 50, from Caelius] (2) On the general political situation I have written often enough — that I don't see peace lasting beyond a year; and the closer the inevitable struggle comes, the more clearly we can see the danger. This is the point over which the leading powers are going to fight: Pompey is determined not to allow Caesar to become consul without first giving up his army and his provinces; but Caesar is convinced that his position will be jeopardized if he leaves his army. His suggestion is that both should give up their armies. . . . (3) In this conflict I see that Pompey will have on his side the Senate and the judiciary, while all those who live a life of fear or desperation will join Caesar, whose army is quite unrivalled. We have quite enough time to assess the resources of both and choose sides. (4) . . . You ask what I think will happen in a few words. Unless one or other of them goes to fight the Parthians, I can see that we are in for a full scale civil war to be decided by violence and the sword.

After his tour of Cisalpine Gaul Caesar returned to supervise the quartering of his legions for the winter. Only one of the nine was left south of the Alps, but even this was enough to start a scare.

379.

(CAESAR) *B.G.* 8.54 (4) This was the division of the army into winter-quarters: Gaius Trebonius was stationed with four legions in Belgium, and another four were sent under Gaius Fabius into the Aedui territory. (5) He thought that Gaul could best be secured if his armies policed the land of the Belgians, who were the best fighters, and of the Aedui, who had the greatest influence. He then left for Italy.

380.

CICERO *ad Att.* 6.9 [Athens, 15 Oct. 50] (5) I am writing this letter on Oct. 15th, the very day on which you say Caesar is bringing four legions to Placentia. What will happen to us, do you think? I am quite happy where I am, in the citadel of Athens.

November 13th, the terminal date approved by Pompey (no. 365), passed unnoticed, and at the beginning of the next month the debate was reopened.

381.

APPIAN *B.C.* 2.30 (118) In the Senate everyone was asked his opinion; [Gaius] Claudius [Marcellus] cleverly divided the question into two and asked separately whether successors should be sent to replace Caesar and whether Pompey should be deprived of his command. Most people voted against the second proposition, but supported the idea of replacing Caesar. (119) Then Curio took the matter further by asking whether they thought both parties ought to give up whatever they commanded; only 22 disapproved, while 370 went back to Curio's proposal as the best way to avoid civil war. 31 (120) Suddenly a false rumour reached them that Caesar had crossed the Alps and was marching on the city. There was great panic and confusion everywhere, and Claudius proposed that the army in Capua should go to face Caesar, as a public enemy. (121) When Curio protested on the ground that the report was untrue, he said 'If the public vote does not allow me to manage affairs as I think best, I shall manage them on my own initiative as consul.' After saying this, he rushed out of the Senate into the suburbs of the city with his colleague and presented a sword to Pompey saying 'My colleague and I bid you march against Caesar on behalf of the country; for this purpose we give you the whole of the present army in Italy — round Capua or anywhere else — and as many other soldiers as you may wish to enlist.' (122) Pompey accepted the consuls' commission, but added 'unless some better way can be found' — a bit of deceitful sophistry intended to put a good face on his actions even then. (123) As it was illegal for tribunes to go outside the walls, Curio's sphere of influence was limited to the city; but he deplored the state of affairs in public and demanded that the consuls should announce that people need pay no attention to Pompey's conscriptions. This achieved nothing and, as his time of office was expiring, he set out hastily to join Caesar, feeling that he could do nothing more to help him and fearing besides for his own safety. 32 (124) Caesar crossed the Alps with 5,000 infantry and 300 horsemen, and descended on Ravenna which marked the end of his province and bordered on Italy. (125) He greeted Curio warmly, thanked him for his services and reviewed the situation.

Caesar's supporters tried to prevail on him to fight it out there and then, but he preferred to negotiate so long as he could keep up the appearance of being the aggrieved party.

382.

SALLUST *Ep. ad Caes.* 3 (1) Either out of a spirit of sheer perversity or an overriding desire to obstruct you, Pompey has sunk so low as to put weapons into the hands of the enemy; you must therefore use the same methods to restore the government as he has to overthrow it. (2) First of all he gave to a few Senators absolute control over revenues, expenditure and judicial matters, leaving the Roman people, who used to have supreme control, enslaved under laws which are not even fair themselves. (3) Even though the courts have, as before, been put into the hands of the three orders, yet the same faction has the power to give or take as it pleases, to defraud the innocent, and to promote its own members.

The authenticity of this letter is in doubt; see M. Gelzer, *Caesar: Politician and Statesman* (Blackwell, 1968) p. 183 n. 1. The tone and context however support its attribution to Sallust who was expelled from the Senate in this year (Dio 40.63.3–64.1).

383.

APPIAN *B.C.* 2.32 (125) Curio's idea was that he should collect his whole army there and then, and march on Rome; but Caesar thought it better to keep trying to negotiate a settlement. (126) So he told his friends to offer these terms on his behalf; that he would give up all the rest of his provinces and armies, keeping only two legions and Illyria with Cisalpine Gaul until he should be elected consul. (127) This satisfied Pompey, but the consuls continued to be obstructive.

384.

(From Caesar's message to Pompey, Dec. 50).

CAESAR *B.C.* 1.9 (2) It made me angry that my enemies should, out of spite, wrest from me a privilege conferred by the Roman people and, robbing me of six months of my command, drag me back to Rome, when the people had decreed that I should be allowed to stand in absence at the next elections.

What six months were these to which Caesar referred?

CICERO'S ANALYSIS

Cicero had returned to Italy in November, but did not go straight to Rome, for fear of being too deeply involved in the conflict. With some reluctance he had already decided to back Pompey in the event of a fight (Cic. *ad Att.* 7.1.4, Oct. 50), but, like many others, he was most in favour of a compromise solution, even if it meant making concessions to Caesar. These letters are the last extant ones written by Cicero before Caesar actually crossed the Rubicon.

Cicero records a talk he had with Pompey on Dec. 10th:

385.

CICERO *ad Att.* 7.4 [Pompeii, 11 Dec. 50] (2) On the political situation he spoke as if war was inevitable. There was no hope of settlement. Of course he had known for some time that Caesar and he were at odds, but he had just received further evidence. Hirtius had just come from Caesar (with whom he was on the closest terms) and had not come to see him; he had arrived on the evening of Dec. 6th, and though Balbus had arranged to meet Scipio before daybreak on the 7th to discuss the whole situation, Hirtius went off to Caesar in the middle of the night. This seemed to Pompey a clear proof of the split. (3) And that's that. My only consoling thought is that he is not likely to be mad enough to endanger his winnings — the second consulship from his enemies and supreme power from fortune.

Cicero is probably referring to the consulship held by Pompey in 52 (see nos. 298 ff.), which was in fact his third.

386.

CICERO *ad Att.* 7.6 [Formiae, 17 Dec. 50] (2) The political situation really frightens me, and I have not found a single person who would prefer to fight rather than give in to Caesar's demands. Certainly the demands are shameless but they have more weight than we thought. Anyway why should we make our first stand now? 'For this evil is no greater' [Homer *Od.* 12.209] than when we gave him a further five years' command, or when we voted him the right to stand for office in absence — unless we were then giving him the weapons which he is now going to use against us (cf. nos **316 ff.**).

387.

CICERO *ad Att.* 7.7 [Formiae, end of Dec. 50] (5) You say that my arrival is most eagerly awaited, and there is not one of the 'good' — or 'good enough' — men in any doubt about what I will do. Who are these 'good men' you talk of? I know of none, no party of such men, that is; there are only a few individuals. When there are policy-disagreements it is parties and groups of good men that we need. Do you call the Senate 'good', when they have left the provinces without governors? (Curio would never have held out if negotiations had been opened with him, but because the Senate rejected the proposal, Caesar has no successor). Or do you mean the tax-collectors who have never been really committed, but are now firm friends of Caesar? Or the financiers and farmers who want nothing so much as peace? Or do you think they would shy away from the prospect of being ruled by a king, when they have shown no signs of doing so as long as they were left in peace?

Pompey and Cicero again met on the afternoon of Dec. 25th at Formiae.

388.

CICERO *ad Att.* 7.8 [Formiae, 26 Dec. 50] (4) In answer to your question whether there is any hope of a peaceful settlement, I can only judge from my long and detailed discussions with Pompey that he doesn't even want any. For he thinks that Caesar will turn everything topsy-turvy even if he is elected consul after dismissing his army; in fact he believes that Caesar will give up the idea of the consulship this year, and will prefer to hang on to his province and army when he hears of the careful preparations being made against him. But if Caesar does lose his head all the same, Pompey feels only the deepest contempt for him, trusting in his own and the state's troops. . . . (5) We had in front of us a public speech delivered by Antony on Dec. 21st; it contained attacks on Pompey since his boyhood, complaints about condemnations and the threat of armed conflict. This was Pompey's reaction — 'What do you think Caesar himself will do if he comes to control the state when his poor wretched quaestor dares to say such things?' In short he seemed not only unwilling to seek peace, but positively afraid of it.

Antony had entered the tribunate on Dec. 10th.

389.

CICERO *ad Att.* 7.9 [Formiae, 26/27 Dec. 50] (2) You must help me solve this problem — political, I need hardly say. The choice is between these alternatives: *a.* Caesar's candidature is admitted, while he retains his army with authority from the Senate or the tribunes; *b.* he is persuaded to accept the consulship on condition of giving up his province and his army; *c.* he cannot be persuaded to do this, and so the elections are held with him forfeiting his candidature, but biding his time and hanging onto his province; *d.* if he will not bide his time, but uses the tribunes to intervene, while taking no violent steps himself, this will lead to an interregnum; *e.* if on the other hand he uses his army in reply to our rejection of his candidature, and we have to fight it out with him, then we may have to face him straightaway when we are still poorly prepared, or later at the elections, when his friends have failed to win their plea that his candidature should be legally admitted—he may justify his resorting to arms either on the simple pretext that his candidature is not admitted, or for the additional reason that a tribune, who has been obstructing the Senate or inciting the people, is censured or bound over by senatorial decree or removed or expelled (or says he has been) and takes refuge with him; once we are committed to war, either we must hold the city, or abandon it and cut him off from his supplies and reinforcements. One of these evils has got to be borne; which do you think is the least intolerable? (3) I have no doubt that you will say that he ought to be persuaded to accept the consulship on condition of giving up his army. Certainly there could be no objection — if he really will submit to this course; in fact I am surprised that he does not, seeing the impossibility of being accepted as a candidate while retaining his army. The objection is that, in some people's opinion, nothing could be worse for us than having him as consul. But you say even that is preferable to his having an army as well. Agreed; but your 'that is preferable' is just what seems to someone [Pompey] the great stumbling-block which cannot be got over. 'Then we must give way to Caesar's wishes.' But just think of his first consulship and then imagine him being consul again. 'Ah yes' you say, 'weak as he then was, he was more than a match for the whole state.' So what do you think he will be like now? Another thing: Pompey is determined to stay in Spain if he is consul. What a tragedy when the worst alternative is one which we cannot refuse and which would immediately win him the highest regard of all the 'good' men if he accepted it. (4) So let us forget about this alternative — which anyway he is said to be most unlikely to accept. Which is the worst of the evils left to us? To accede to the demand which Pompey claims is the most shameless of all? You have held a province for a period of ten years which was given you not by the Senate but by your own hand, backed by the violence of your faction; the period determined not by law, but by your capricious will — still, let us call it determined by law — has expired. A successor is decreed. You butt in and say 'What about me and my candidature?' What about us? Do you mean to hang onto your army longer than the people have stipulated, in defiance of the Senate? 'You must fight to the end — or give in.' Then, as Pompey says, let us fight with a good hope of victory or die with freedom. Now if we do have to fight, chance will determine when, the circumstances will determine how. So I won't tax you with answering that problem; but let me know what your reactions are to what I have said. I tell you, I am tortured day and night.

Cicero's analysis still leaves some questions to be answered; for instance he does not make it clear who, in his opinion, bears the major responsibility for a state of affairs in which war is apparently inevitable. Though distressed by Caesar's 'demands' (no. 386), he accepts that they may be justifiable and is more critical of the Senate which refuses to negotiate (no. 387). His attitude to Pompey is ambivalent: although he makes repeated references to Pompey's militancy (nos. 385, 388), he does not criticize it, presumably because he was already committed to following Pompey's lead himself. A politician of the opposite side asserts quite categorically that Pompey's behaviour is illegal and must be forcibly suppressed (no. 382). Later writers, able to view the events dispassionately, tend to take Caesar's side: he refused to take offence over the recall of his legion and tried to negotiate a settlement (nos. 369, 372, 383) whereas Pompey got little credit from the incident (nos. 371, 373). The consuls are no less criticized (no. 383), in particular Gaius Marcellus, who on his own initiative entrusted the military command to Pompey (nos. 374, 381). As a body, the members of the Senate seem the least anxious to provoke a conflict (nos. 363, 366, 374, 381), but perhaps at a time like this their very willingness to accommodate both sides may be reckoned a fault (nos. 374, 378). How then should the blame be shared? What alternatives were there to armed conflict, and why were they not acceptable?

B. The last days

By the beginning of the new year (49) it was evident that no one was going to make any significant concessions. The issue would only be settled by arms, and in the few days before the first blow was struck both sides looked around to find justifications for their decision to fight. There was no obvious way of establishing the constitutional rights and wrongs. Caesar could claim that he was protected by the Law of the Ten Tribunes (nos. 316 ff.) and by the vetoes which the Senate had upheld (no. 366); his intervention was justified by the need to defend the rights of the tribunes. The Senate countered this by passing the 'Ultimate Decree' (see no. 294 n.) which authorized their taking up arms on the ground that they were defending the Republic from harm. How are the merits of the two cases to be determined? From the historical accounts which survive, the person who seems to come out worst is Pompey, perhaps because he did not live to qualify for the apologies and eulogies which were heaped upon the victorious Caesar.

CAESAR'S LETTER TO THE SENATE

390.
CICERO *ad Fam.* 16.11 [near Rome, 12 Jan. 49, to Tiro] (2) In short our friend Caesar has sent a threatening and bad-tempered letter to the Senate and is shameless enough to hang onto his army and province in defiance of the Senate, but with the encouragement of my old friend Curio.

> Would Cicero be using the term 'old friend' literally or sarcastically — or in both senses? See Index, under Scribonius Curio.

391.

SUETONIUS *Div. Jul.* 29 (2) Seeing the relentless march of events, and the potential opposition of the consuls designate as well, Caesar wrote to the Senate asking them not to take away a privilege conferred by the people, or at any rate to ensure that the other generals left their armies too; presumably he was confident that he could collect his veterans as soon as he wanted them, more easily than Pompey could muster his recruits. He also suggested to his adversaries an arrangement whereby he should relinquish Transalpine Gaul and eight legions, keeping only two and the Cisalpine province, or even just one with the command of Illyricum, until he became consul.

> Caesar could afford to offer such a compromise since the size of his province now mattered less to him than the protection provided by holding a provincial command.

392.

APPIAN *B.C.* 2.32 (127) Caesar then wrote a letter to the Senate and entrusted it to Curio, who covered the distance of 2,300 stades [= c.270 miles] in three days and delivered it to the new consuls as they were entering the Senate House on New Year's Day. (128) The letter contained a dignified recital of all Caeser's achievements since the beginning and a declaration that he was prepared to lay down his command at the same time as Pompey; he would not do so while Pompey retained his, but would soon arrive to avenge the insults done to his country and himself. (129) This was received with uproar, as if it were a declaration of war, and everyone shouted that Lucius Domitius should be his successor. Domitius at once took the field with 4,000 reserves.

393.

CAESAR *B.C.* 1.1 (1) Caesar's letter was delivered to the consuls, but it was only with the greatest of difficulty that the tribunes managed to persuade them to read it out in the Senate; even then they did not succeed in tabling a motion about its contents, (2) as the consuls put before the House a sweeping motion about the general situation. The consul Lucius Lentulus promised the Senate that he would not fail the state if they were prepared to make a bold and brave decision; (3) but if they tried to ingratiate themselves with Caesar, as they had done before, by taking his wishes into consideration, then he would take the initiative himself and pay no attention to the recommendations of the Senate, as he too could take refuge in the friendship and favour of Caesar. (4) Scipio took the same line in his speech; he said that Pompey did not intend to fail the state, so long as the Senate would follow him; but if they were hesitant or half-hearted, there would be no point in their coming to beg help from him later on. 2 (1) It looked as if Scipio was simply acting as the mouthpiece of Pompey, who was no distance away from Rome where the Senate was meeting ... (2) Other speakers were Marcus Marcellus who suggested the immediate conscription of an army to protect the state, (3) and Marcus Calidius who proposed that Pompey should go to his province; [but Lentulus prevented either of these suggestions being put to the vote] ... (6) So the words of the consul, the fear of the nearby army, and the threats of Pompey's friends compelled most of them against their will to accept the proposal of Scipio: that Caesar should dismiss his army before a fixed date on pain of being outlawed. (7) The tribunes Marcus Antonius and Quintus Cassius interposed a veto; and at once the matter of their veto was put before the Senate.

THE RETURN OF CICERO

Cicero returned to Rome on Jan. 4th, but his hopes of making peace were dashed by the refusal of Pompey and Lentulus to make concessions.

394.
CICERO *ad Fam.* 16.12 [Capua, 27 Jan. 49, to Tiro] (2) Ever since I returned to Rome, all my thoughts, utterances, and actions have been directed towards a peaceful settlement; but an obsessive mania for fighting has got into everyone — not only the subversive elements but even those who are regarded as loyal citizens — though I was crying out that there was no misery greater than civil war.

Cicero expressed similar sentiments in a letter to Sulpicius Rufus, whom he saw as another potential peacemaker (*ad Fam.* 4.4.1, April 49).

395.

CICERO *ad Fam.* 6.6 [Rome, Sept. 46, to Aulus Caecina] (5) I would not like Caesar, who has deserved so well of me, to think that I gave Pompey advice which, if followed, would have meant that Caesar would not be enjoying his present power — though I dare say he would still have been of great eminence and distinction in civilian life. My opinion was that Pompey ought to go to Spain; if he had done so, there would have been no question of a civil war. As for the question of candidature in absence, I did not fight to have it legalized, but rather that it should be accepted, as the people had sanctioned it with the militant support of the consul himself.

396.

CICERO *ad Att.* 9.11a [Formiae, 19 March 49, to Caesar] (2) From the earliest opportunity, I have always tried to promote a peaceful settlement with Pompey and the Senate, and since hostilities began I have played no part in the fighting. It seemed to me that you were the injured party in the war, as your enemies out of spite were trying to take away an honour conferred on you by the favour of the Roman people.

How sincere was Cicero being? Compare the sentiments in no. **390.**

397.

PLUTARCH *Pomp.* 59 (3) Cicero, recently returned from Cilicia, tried to arrange a settlement whereby Caesar would leave Gaul and give up the rest of his army except for two legions and retain Illyria while he waited for his second consulship. (4) As Pompey continued to object, Caesar's friends agreed to his giving up one of the two legions; but Lentulus still opposed it, and Cato loudly declared that Pompey was going astray again through having the wool pulled over his eyes; so the negotiations came to nothing.

For Caesar's continued interest in Illyria, see nos. **86 ff., 136 ff.**

398.

VELLEIUS 2.49 (3) Caesar tried everything he could to keep the peace, but no offer was acceptable to the Pompeians. Of the consuls, one was unreasonably savage, the other, Lentulus, could not protect himself and the state at the same time; Marcus Cato declared that it was better for the Republic to die than to accept any terms from a solitary citizen.

THE ULTIMATE DECREE AND FLIGHT OF THE TRIBUNES

399.

CAESAR *B.C.* 1.5 (3) They turned to their final expedient, the ultimate decree of the Senate, which had never before been resorted to except in dire emergencies when the wanton misuse of power had brought the city to the verge of destruction: 'Let the consuls, praetors, tribunes, and proconsuls do what is in their power to see that no harm befalls the Republic.' (4) This decree was passed on Jan. 7th. . . . (5) At once the tribunes fled from the city to take refuge with Caesar. At this moment he was at Ravenna, waiting for an answer to his very mild demands, in the hope that people's sense of fair play would bring the matter to a peaceful conclusion.

400.

CICERO *ad Fam.* 16.11 [near Rome, 12 Jan. 49, to Tiro] (2) Our friend Antony and Quintus Cassius, although they were not forcibly expelled, set out with Curio to join Caesar after the Senate had imposed on the consuls, praetors, tribunes, and us ex-consuls the task of seeing that 'the Republic suffered no harm'.

> This contemporary testimony seems to make it quite clear that the tribunes fled of their own accord. Certainly they could no longer expect to wield any effective power in Rome, but there were apparently no grounds for the myth of expulsion which even Caesar adopted as a justification of his recourse to arms.

401.

APPIAN *B.C.* 2.33 (130) Antonius and Cassius succeeded Curio as tribunes and shared his sympathies; this made the Senate even more frantic, and they declared Pompey's army to be the guardian of Rome and Caesar's to be a public enemy. (131) The consuls Marcellus and Lentulus told Antonius and his colleagues to stay away from the Senate in case anything untoward should happen to them, tribunes though they were. With an angry shout Antony leapt up from his seat and called on the gods to witness the insults being heaped on his sacred and inviolable office; they were being driven out in contempt, though they had committed no murder or profanity, but were simply expressing the opinions which they thought to be to the public good. (132) After saying this he rushed out like one possessed, prophesying wars, massacres, proscriptions, banishment, confiscation and all the other misfortunes they were going to suffer, calling down fearful imprecations on those responsible. Curio and Cassius left with him, as some of Pompey's army was already to be seen standing round the Senate House. (133) They went to Caesar the same night with all speed, disguised as slaves and using a hired carriage to escape detection. Caesar showed them to his army just as they were, and in a rousing speech described how men with their record were being regarded as enemies and the people who dared to say a word on their behalf were being driven out in disgrace.

402.

PLUTARCH *Ant.* 5 (4) When Caesar's friends brought forward a further set of demands which seemed to be reasonable, Cato still objected and the consul Lentulus expelled Antony from the Senate.

403.

SUETONIUS *Div. Jul.* 30 (1) As the Senate made no move to intervene in the dispute and his opponents declared that they would accept no compromise in a matter of such national importance, Caesar crossed into Cisalpine Gaul; after making a tour of duty, he halted at Ravenna, determining to punish by arms any attempt by the Senate to suppress the tribunes who interposed vetoes on his behalf.

404.

CAESAR *B.C.* 1.7 (8) The soldiers of the 13th legion (which had been called out at the first news of the trouble and had arrived before any of the others) declared that they were ready to seek redress for the wrongs done to their general and to the tribunes of the people. 8 (1) After discovering the inclination of his soldiers, he set out with that legion to Ariminum, where he met the tribunes who had fled to him. The other legions were summoned from their winter-quarters and ordered to follow.

The 12th legion joined him at Cingulum in Picenum (*B.C.* 1.15.3); the 8th, with 22 new cohorts levied in Gaul and 300 horsemen from Noricum, in Corfinium (*B.C.* 1.18.5).

Caesar had a midnight conference in front of Corfinium with Lentulus Spinther (cons. 57).

405.

CAESAR *B.C.* 1.22 (5) Caesar interrupted him in the middle of his remarks, saying that he had left his province not for any evil purposes, but to protect himself from the insulting behaviour of his enemies, to restore to their proper position the tribunes who had been expelled from the state over this business (see no. **400** n.) and to liberate and avenge the Roman people from the oppression of a minority faction.

> Most of our sources follow this Caesarian line — see e.g. nos. **392, 398, 402.** What would the main counter arguments of a senatorial spokesman have been?

THE RUBICON

406.

VELLEIUS 2.49 (4) Finally when all Caesar's demands had been scornfully rejected (although he would have been happy to retain his title to a province, with only one legion), the Senate decreed that he should enter the city without office and should put himself in the hands of the electorate in his candidature for the consulship. From this Caesar concluded that war was the only answer, and with his army he crossed the Rubicon.

407.

APPIAN *B.C.* 2.34 (134) The war had now begun on both sides and had been openly declared. The Senate, thinking that Caesar would take a little time to collect his army from Gaul and would not rush into such an enterprise with only a few troops, ordered Pompey to collect an army of 130,000 Italians (including as many as possible veterans with war service behind them) and to enlist the strongest body of troops he could from the neighbouring provinces. (135) To finance the war they at once voted that he should have all the contents of the public treasury and their private fortunes as well if the expenses of the army required it. They also sent round for further contributions from the allied cities, leaving no stone unturned in their indignation and eagerness for victory. (136) Caesar had sent round to collect his own army, but as he relied more upon his speed and daring to effect surprise and panic than upon overwhelming preparations, he decided to take the initiative in this great war by using his five thousand men to capture the key points of Italy first. 35 (137) So he sent forward his centurions and a few particularly fearless troops, not dressed for war, telling them to enter Ariminum — the first town in Italy beyond the frontier with Gaul — and to take it by surprise. (138) He himself, around evening, excused himself from a banquet on the plea of not feeling well, left his friends still feasting and drove by chariot to Ariminum with the cavalry following a little way behind. (139) When he reached the river Rubicon, which forms the boundary with Italy, and gazed out over the stream, he was lost in thought, contemplating all the evils that would follow if he crossed this river with his army. (140) Then, coming to himself again, he said to his companions 'If I fail to cross this river, it will be the beginning of many miseries for me; if I do cross, it will bring misery to everyone.' With these words he put an end to his hesitation and crossed like a man possessed, pronouncing as he did so the familiar phrase: 'There — the die is cast.'

The Rubicon-crossing episode captured the imagination of many ancient writers, and other accounts contain a wealth of incidental detail of variable reliability:

Plutarch *Caes.* 32. says that Asinius Pollio was among his companions on the bank of the stream with whom he discussed the grave consequences of his crossing.

Plutarch *Pomp.* 60. puts the number of his escorting cavalry at 300 and says that the words 'The die is cast' (lit. 'Let the dice have been cast') were spoken in Greek.

Suetonius *Div. Jul.* 31–32. has Caesar say 'Even now, we can turn back; but once we cross this little bridge, there is no alternative but war' (31.2). His hesitancy was resolved by an apparition who took a trumpet from one of Caesar's men, sounded the call to arms and strode across to the opposite side.

Two retrospective judgements to be compared:

408.

SUETONIUS *Div. Jul.* 30 (2) Pompey used often to say that Caesar wanted everything reduced to confusion as his private means were inadequate for completing the project he had undertaken or for fulfilling the expectations that the people had been given of his return. (3) Others say that he had been frightened at the thought of having to render account for all that he had done in his first consulship in the face of auspices, laws, and vetoes; Marcus Cato had in fact been declaring repeatedly that he would prosecute him as soon as he disbanded his army. It was common talk that if he had to come back without office, he would plead his case in front of the judges surrounded by an armed bodyguard like Milo. (4) This is made more likely by the remark reported by Asinius Pollio; he says that when Caesar surveyed the enemy dead or in flight at the battle of Pharsalus, these were his actual words; 'This was what they wanted. For all my achievements I, Gaius Caesar, would have been condemned, had I not sought help from my army.' (5) Some think that his familiarity with power became an obsession and that, after weighing his own resources against those of his opponents, he took this opportunity of seizing the supremacy he had longed for all his life. Cicero seems to have been of this opinion; in his work 'on Duties' he says that Caesar always had on his lips these lines of Euripides (of which he offered a translation of his own):

'For if right is to be violated, let it be violated for the sake of becoming king. In other things let piety be observed'.

409.

CICERO *ad Att.* 8.11 [Formiae, 27 Feb. 49]

[Cicero begins the letter by describing how he spends the time in philo-sophic contemplation of the ideal statesman; such a man is described in the fifth book of his *Republic* as being one whose aim is to secure a happy life for his citizens.]

(2) Such an idea never entered our friend Gnaius' head in the past and it certainly hasn't in the present situation. Both of them are looking for supreme power, and their aim is not to make the state honoured and happy. I tell you, his reason for leaving the city was

not his inability to defend it, and he did not leave Italy because he was driven out; his first thought was to stir up every land and every sea, to invite barbarian kings to war, to bring armed hordes of savages into Italy and to collect the largest possible armies. He is one among many similarly inclined whose aim is a kind of Sullan regime. Do you think that there is no understanding between them, that no agreement has ever been possible? Today there is a possibility. But neither of them has our happiness as their aim. They both want to be kings.

Bibliography

Some of the more recent works published in English:

BOOKS

Adcock, F. E., *Marcus Crassus, Millionaire* (Heffer, 1967).
Balsdon, J. P. V. D., *Julius Caesar and Rome* (E.U.P., 1967).
Dickson, J., *Death of a Republic. Politics and Political Thought at Rome* 59–44 *B.C.* (N.Y., Macmillan, 1963).
Fuller, J. F. C., *Julius Caesar, Man, Soldier and Tyrant* (Eyre and Spottiswoode, 1965).
Gelzer, M., *Caesar, Politician and Statesman* (Blackwell, 1968).
Smith, R. E., *The Failure of the Roman Republic* (C.U.P., 1955).
Taylor, L. R., *Party Politics in the Age of Caesar* (Berk. Univ. 1949).

ARTICLES

Caesar's consulship
Balsdon, 'Roman History 65–50 B.C. Five problems: the *publicani* and Asia' *JRS* LII (1962), 134–41.
Grummel, W. C., 'The consular elections of 59 B.C.' *CJ* XLIX (1953–4), 351–5.
Smith, 'The significance of Caesar's consulship in 59 B.C.' *Phoenix* XVIII (1964), 303–313.
Taylor, 'The date and meaning of the Vettius affair' *Historia* I (1950), 45–51.
Taylor, 'On the chronology of Caesar's first consulship' *AJPh* LXXII (1951), 254–68.

Clodius
Balsdon, 'Roman History 58–56 B.C. Three Ciceronian problems: Clodius' abrogation of the *Lex Aelia Fufia*' *JRS* XLVII (1957), 15–20.

Gruen, E. S., 'P. Clodius, instrument or independent agent' *Phoenix* XX (1966), 120–30.

Lintott, A. W., 'P. Clodius Pulcher. *Felix Catilina* ?' *Greece and Rome* (*NS*) XIV (1967), 157–69.

Oost, S. I., 'Cato Uticensis and the annexation of Cyprus' *CPh* L (1955), 98–112.

Rowland, R. J., 'Crassus, Clodius and Curio in the year 59 B.C.' *Historia* XV (1966), 217–23.

Seager, R., 'Clodius, Pompeius and the exile of Cicero' *Latomus* XXIV (1965), 519–31.

Conference of Luca

Balsdon, 'Three Ciceronian problems: Cicero and the *Lex Campana* in 56' *JRS* XLVII (1957), 15–20.

Balsdon, 'Five problems: Caesar's requests in 56, and Cicero's palinode; provinces for the consuls of 55' *JRS* LII (1962), 134–41.

Gruen, 'Pompey, the Roman aristocracy, and the Conference of Luca' *Historia* XVIII (1969), 71–108.

Lazenby, J. F., 'The Conference of Luca and the Gallic War' *Latomus* XVIII (1959), 67–76.

Stevens, C. E., 'Britain and the *Lex Pompeia Licinia*' *Latomus* XII (1953), 14–21.

Pompey

Balsdon, 'Three Ciceronian Problems: Pompey and *maius imperium* in 57' *JRS* XLVII (1957), 15–20.

Collins, H. P., 'Decline and Fall of Pompey the Great' *Greece and Rome* XXII (1953), 98–106.

Pocock, L. G., 'What made Pompeius fight in 49 B.C. ?' *Greece and Rome* (*NS*) VI (1959), 68–81.

Termination of Caesar's command

Balsdon, 'Five problems: *Absentis ratio*' *JRS* LII (1962), 134–41.

Cuff, P. J., 'The terminal date of Caesar's command' *Historia* VII (1958), 445–71.

Lacey, W. K., 'The tribunate of Curio' *Historia* X (1961), 318–29.

Brief Notes on the Authors and
Works Quoted

AMMIANUS Marcellinus (4th cent. A.D.) from Antioch; wrote a history of events from 96 to 378 A.D.

APPIAN, (2nd cent. A.D.) from Alexandria; wrote a series of monographs on areas conquered by the Romans, e.g. books on the Celtic (*Celt.*) and Illyrian (*Ill.*) wars; and on the Civil Wars of Rome (*B.C.*). Much of his information is derived ultimately from respectable literary and annalistic sources, but is tainted in transmission by dependence on more recent imperial writers.

ASCONIUS Pedianus, Q. (9 B.C.–76 A.D.); wrote historical commentaries on Cicero's speeches, deriving his information from Cicero's own writing. References are to page numbers in the *Oxford Classical Text* edited by A. C. Clark.

AUGUSTUS, C. Julius Caesar (63 B.C.–14 A.D.), Emperor; compiled a record of all the achievements of his Principate (*Res Gestae*).

CAESAR, C. Julius (?100–44 B.C.); wrote seven books of 'Commentaries' on the Gallic Wars of 59–50 (*B.G.*) — the eighth was written by his lieutenant Aulus Hirtius; and three on the Civil Wars of 49–48 (*B.C.*). For his limitations as a historical source, see Introd. to ch. III.

CATULLUS, C. Valerius (c.84–54 B.C.) from Verona; much of his love-poetry directed at Clodius' sister; for his hostility to Caesar see nos. **234–5.**

CICERO, M. Tullius (106–43 B.C.); his writing provides the best contemporary evidence for political events of 60–50, but its reliability is less when he has a special case to plead (see e.g. introd. to no. **177**) and is not just recording information. It should also be remembered that the speeches we possess are almost certainly not as delivered but have been rewritten by Cicero with a view to publication.

Speeches (arranged by years):

57 To the Senate on his return from exile (*post red. in Sen.*); a eulogy of Pompey and the Senate, with an attack on Clodius and the consuls of 58.

On his House (*Dom.*); a plea that the decree of banishment and confiscation of his goods was invalidated by the illegality of Clodius' tribunate.

56 (Feb.) Successful defence of P. Sestius (*Sest.*), tr. 57, against whom Clodius brought charges of bribery and assault. Cic. was only one of the defence counsel, and his speech dealt with the political background to the charges. It included a specific attack on Vatinius, tr. 59, (*Vat.*), who was one of the prosecution witnesses.

On the allocation of provinces to the consuls of 55 (*Prov. Cos.*) under the *Lex Sempronia*.

In defence of L. Cornelius Balbus, a Knight and agent of Caesar (*Balb.*), charged with usurping citizenship (which had in fact been granted to him by Pompey in Spain for fighting against Sertorius). Cicero, Pompey, and Crassus all helped to get him acquitted.

55 A bitter attack on Piso, cons. 58, (*Pis.*), whose misgovernment of his Macedonian province Cicero had earlier criticized in *Prov. Cos.*

54 (Dec.) Successful defence of C. Rabirius Postumus (*Rab. Post.*), a wealthy Knight involved in Gabinius' expedition to Egypt (see nos. **244** ff.). A significant portion of the speech is taken up with a eulogy of Caesar, whose dependant Rabirius was.

52 For the circumstances of the speech on behalf of T. Annius Milo (*Mil.*) see nos. **290–309** (esp. **307**).

Schol. Bob.: notes on Cicero's speeches compiled at the Italian monastery of Bobbio, which was founded in the 7th century.

Letters

To T. Pomponius Atticus (*ad Att.*), a very rich banking friend who managed to preserve a strict political neutrality.

To Friends (*ad Fam.*), this series includes some written *to* Cicero (see no. **336** n.).

To his brother Quintus (*ad Q.F.*), who was proconsul in Asia 62–58, a legate of Pompey in Sardinia 57–56, and of Caesar in Britain and Gaul 54–52.

Philosophical Works

The Tusculan Disputations (*Tusc.*), based on a series of conversations with friends, written in 46; Bk. I is about the fear of death.

DIO Cassius of Bithynia, praetor in 193 A.D.; wrote a complete Roman History, of which the books covering the period 60–50 B.C. are fully preserved. Knowing nothing of Republican institutions, he drew heavily on Livy for information. He is important because he is often the only source, but his judgement is based on an imperial viewpoint.

DIO CHRYSOSTOM, born c. 40 A.D. in Bithynia; during a period of exile he absorbed the Cynic philosophy and later wrote a large number of speeches based on this doctrine.

FLORUS, ?Lucius Annaeus (early 2nd cent. A.D.); wrote an Epitome of Roman military history, drawn largely from Livy.

JORDANES, a Gothic monk of the 6th cent. A.D. who wrote a history of his own people (*Get.*); much of his information is drived from Cassiodorus who a century earlier had supervised the compilation of numerous Italian historical manuscripts.

LIVY (T. Livius, 59 B.C.–17 A.D.); wrote a history of Rome in 142 volumes. For the period 60–50 B.C. only a brief summary (the *Periochae*) survives, and his work is more important as supplying the material for later writers. As the period was nearly within his own experience and as his information came largely from contemporary sources, he was probably a reliable authority even though his account must have been coloured by his belief in the moral decline of the Republic.

OROSIUS (early 5th cent. A.D.); a Spanish Christian who wrote a history of Rome largely derived from Livy.

OVID (P. Ovidius Naso, 43 B.C.–18 A.D.); banished in 8 A.D. when half way through the *Fasti*, a work which incorporated history and legend under the appropriate day of the year.

PLINY the Elder (C. Plinius Secundus, 23–79 A.D.); his Natural History (*N.H.*) is a massive, totally uncritical compilation of factual information from over 450 different authors.

PLUTARCH (c. 50–120 A.D.) from Chaeronea; among his enormous literary output is a series of biographies comparing Greek and Roman characters, e.g. Caesar and Alexander; as his primary concern is with moral problems, he is not very critical of his sources (usually Greek and second-hand), but he read widely and often quotes the author.

SALLUST (C. Sallustius Crispus, tr. 52); for his letter to Caesar (*Ep. ad Caes.*), see no. **382** n.

STRABO, born c. 64 B.C. in Pontus; as well as some lost historical works, wrote a 'Geography' comprising mostly second hand information and perhaps compiled for a political rather than a scientific purpose.

SUETONIUS Tranquillus, C. (c. 70–140 A.D.); for a time secretary to the Emperor Hadrian, and thus had access to imperial archives; wrote a series of 'Lives of the Caesars' from Julius (*Div. Jul.*) to Domitian; collected his material methodically and is of particular value where he quoted non-literary sources; but his judgement is unreliable because he does not differentiate between the authority of the sources he draws on.

TACITUS, P. Cornelius (c. 55 – c. 115 A.D.); wrote a eulogistic monograph on his father-in-law, Cn. Julius Agricola, who was governor of Britain for six years (77/78 – 83/84 A.D.).

VELLEIUS Paterculus, C., praetor in 15 A.D.; wrote a Roman History of which Bk. 2 covers the period 146 B.C. to 30 A.D.; a soldier rather than a serious historian, staunchly loyal to the imperial dynasty.

Inscriptions

I.L.S.: Latin inscriptions selected and edited by Dessau.

S.I.G.[4]: Greek inscriptions selected and edited by Dittenberger (4th edition).

SALONA DECREE: published by R. Rendić-Miočević in *Studii Aquileiesi* (1953) pp. 67–81.

Index of Passages

Index of Persons

All dates are in brackets; all references are to the numbered excerpts in the book, *not* to page-numbers.

The names of Caesar and Pompey are abbreviated to C. and P. respectively, and should not be confused with the abbreviations for the fore-names Gaius and Publius.

Other abbreviations:

> aed. = aedile
> cens. = censor
> cons. = consul
> pr. = praetor
> qu. = quaestor
> tr. = tribune of the people